71 Coltn

T0228566

Richar

methuen | drama

LONDON • NEW YORK • OXFORD • NEW DELHI • SYDNEY

METHUEN DRAMA
Bloomsbury Publishing Plc
50 Bedford Square, London, WC1B 3DP, UK
1385 Broadway, New York, NY 10018, USA
29 Earlsfort Terrace, Dublin 2, Ireland

BLOOMSBURY, METHUEN DRAMA and the Methuen
Drama logo are trademarks of Bloomsbury Publishing Plc

First published in Great Britain 2022 by Methuen Drama

Cover design by Ben Anslow
Cover image © Bob King Creative

A catalogue record for this book is available from the British Library.

A catalog record for this book is available from the Library of Congress.

ISBN: PB: 978-1-3503-4212-5
ePDF: 978-1-3503-4213-2
eBook: 978-1-3503-4214-9

Series: Modern Plays

Typeset by Mark Heslington Ltd, Scarborough, North Yorkshire

To find out more about our authors and books visit
www.bloomsbury.com and sign up for our newsletters.

71 Coltman Street premiered at Hull Truck Theatre on 22 February 2022 with the following cast and creative team.

Cast (*in order of appearance*)

Lauryn Redding	Linda
Laurie Jamieson	Stew
Joanna Holden	Mrs Snowball / Camo
Adrian Hood	Our Seth
Kieran Knowles	Mike Bradwell
Jordan Metcalfe	Julian
Hanna Khogali	Bea
Matthew Booth	Graham Burke / Daz / Howard Gibbins
Jack Chamberlain	Taxi Driver / Police Officer
Annie Kirkman	Samantha / Understudy

Creative Team

Written by	Richard Bean
Directed by	Mark Babych
Composer	Richard Thomas
Musical Director	Sonum Batra
Set & Costume Design	Sara Perks
Lighting Design	Charlie Morgan Jones
Sound Design	Adam P McCready
Casting Director	Annelie Powell
Casting Assistant	Sarah Harkins
Assistant Director	Hannah Stone

Production Team

Producer	Adam Pownall
Production Manager	Oliver Brown
Production Sound	Tom Smith
Lighting Programmer	Jessie Addinall

Stage Management

Company Stage Manager	Shona Wright
Deputy Stage Manager	Jane Williamson
Assistant Stage Manager (book cover)	Laura Alexander-Smith

Scenic

Master Carpenter	Chris Bewers
Carpenter	Dan Lewis
Scenic Artists	Rory David & Ian Hinley
Props Maker	Mark Kesteven
Fabrication	W Campbells & Son

Wardrobe

Head of Wardrobe	Siân Thomas
Wig & Make-up Supervisor	Laura Wilson
Wardrobe Maintenance	Molly Frankland

Thanks . . .

I'd like to thank Mike Bradwell for helping me in the research for this play. He also took over the writing on a couple of occasions when I was stuck to discover what he might say in any given scene. Mike just wrote the speech and sent it to me. Mostly, I'd put it in virtually unchanged.

In researching the play I interviewed some of the early Truckers, and I am indebted to them, stealing their stories and insights.

Linda Bell (Rachel Bell for Equity) supplied me with archive materials and her own memories. As Mike's partner in the early days she was also able to fill me in on the emotional life of the house.

Thurston Binns, as the sound man/roadie for Truck, helped me with early recordings of the plays and the cabaret, and a steady stream of stories.

Anecdotes and local colour were supplied by Mia Soteriou, David Threlfall, Alan Williams and Pete Nicholson.

Robin Soans supplied more than stories, he kindly allowed his vicar's sermon to be reproduced.

I didn't interview every Trucker and if I need to apologise for that then I do. Steve Halliwell, John Lee, Mark Allain, Cass Patton, Mary East and Jim Broadbent are names I know, but there are many others.

Finally, on behalf of my home city of Hull, thank you for setting up an experimental theatre company here, putting us on the cultural map, and leaving such a creative and positive legacy.

The Rent

As the audience enter 'Dark Star' from the 'Live Dead' (Grateful Dead) album plays. It is being played on a Dansette record player which someone has cabled up to a larger valve radio with a bigger speaker. (The track is over twenty minutes long so can play throughout.)

On the sofa sit **Linda** *and* **Stew**, *one cushion apart.* **Stew** *is rolling, creating a six Rizla joint, using the album cover as a surface, breaking cigarettes for the tobacco. He has long hair, green loon pants, a cheesecloth shirt, and a bell around his neck.* **Linda** *is dressed in a tie dye T-shirt and Indian-styled maxi dress with beads and long hair. She is plucking away at an acoustic guitar, and occasionally eating crisps and drinking from a can of Long Life. A second can of Long Life sits on the cable bobbin coffee table.*

Linda Astral? Astral? Astral?

She reaches over and rings the bell around his neck.

Stew What?

Linda What yer doing?

Stew Ori-fucking-gami.

Linda We don't have any dope.

Stew I'll go out.

Linda You? You can't get decent dope in Hull.

Stew I can get Lebanese Red for sixteen quid an ounce.

Linda Where can you get Lebanese Red for sixteen quid?

Stew The Lebanon.

Linda You've never been to the Lebanon.

Stew Lighthouse, down the Flamingo, he can get decent Leb Red.

Linda   Lighthouse can't get Leb Red for sixteen quid an ounce.

Stew   He can for me.

Linda   He can't for me.

Stew   He can for me.

Linda   He can't for me.

Stew   You don't know him.

Linda   Fucking do.

Stew   Fucking don't.

Linda   Fucking do.

Stew   Fucking don't.

Linda   'kin do.

Stew   'kin don't. How long have you known him?

Linda   Seven years.

Stew   Eight years.

Linda   Have you got sixteen quid?

Stew   Have I fuck. And I'm saving up to see Slim Whitman.

Linda   Who the fuck's Slim Whitman?

Stew   You've heard of Slim Whitman. 'The Yodelling Cowboy'?

Linda   He's a yodelling cowboy?

Stew   He does a bit of yodelling, yeah. He's coming to Hull.

Linda   Because that's what Hull really needs, a yodelling fucking cowboy.

Stew   We could put our bread together, and I could go out, and score a three quid deal. Flamingo.

Linda   You're not homosexual, they won't let you in.

71 Coltman Street

Set

A large ground floor room in 71 Coltman Street. A single bed stage left; a sofa, up stage right; a fire place set in the stage right wall, with a fire still burning. Up stage centre, a door to the hall. The room is littered with 'found' wooden chairs ready for the fire, and a cable bobbin serves as a coffee table. By the bed is a wooden pallet. Down stage right, on the street, a white/cream coloured phone box. The bare floorboards have bits of rubber-backed carpet, possibly disparate samples, trying and failing to perform the function of a carpet. A very large beaten up armchair is set with its back to the audience against the wall stage right and facing the sofa. An electric fan heater, not working, is plugged into the wall. There is an acoustic guitar, electric guitar, tambourine, and a bass guitar and amp kicking around.

For the second half a theatre curtain is employed to differentiate between the naturalistic set of Coltman Street and the cabaret or theatre venues of the second half.

Structure

The Rent

The Truck

Interval

The Cabaret

Repercussions

The Play

The Critics

Characters

Mike Bradwell, *twenty-four*
Stew, *twenty-two*
Julian, *twenty-two*
Linda, *twenty-two*
Beatrice (Bea), *twenty-two*
Mrs Snowball, *sixties*
Our Seth, *forties*
Camilla (Camo), *twenty-two*
Police Officer, *twenty-five*
Graham Burke, *forties*
Hell's Angel, *forties*
Howard Gibbins, *forties*
Police Officer, *thirties*

The actor playing **Graham Burke**, *can double as* **Howard Gibbins**, *the* **Police Officer** *and the* **Hell's Angel**.

The actor playing **Mrs Snowball** *can double as* **Camo**.

Songs

'Fan Heater' and 'To The Stars' lyrics were created by early Truckers, with original music by Richard Thomas.

All other original songs have lyrics by Richard Bean and Richard Thomas with music by Richard Thomas.

Stew   I'll dress like one, yeah, and tell them I'm into men, you know, big time, at the door. Giss yer money.

Linda   I need my money for my egg.

Stew   Your egg?

Linda   I have a boiled egg every morning.

Stew   Where can you buy one egg?

Linda   Joan's. Joan sells me one egg and one cigarette.

Stew   Man, that is not a healthy breakfast.

Linda   What's wrong with eggs?

Stew   Cholesterol. I was in that health shop on Prinny Ave and there was this amazing chick in there and she was really laying it on me about cigarettes, and all the tar and nicotine and shit, man.

Linda   I suppose she grows her own muesli.

Stew   She actually moved to Hull so she could live on a ley line.

Linda   There's a ley line in Hull?

Stew   Yeah, Marlborough Ave.

Linda   I'm thinking of getting into health foods 'cause at the end of the day, man, they've got to be better for, you know, your health.

The door opens and **Mrs Snowball** *enters followed by her son,* **Seth**. **Linda** *and* **Stew**, *pause, but don't acknowledge them.* **Mrs Snowball** *is a woman of about sixty-five.* **Seth** *is massive, with mooncalf mannerisms, and about forty, wearing galoshes and a trench coat.* **Seth** *is carrying a spade and a dead Alsatian dog, which he holds by the tail.* **Mrs Snowball** *looks at the armchair, and then at the sofa.* **Linda** *looks at the armchair and carries on.*

Linda   I've only got two quid.

Stew   Giss it, baby.

She hands over two one pound notes, actually monopoly money. **Seth** *walks forward and stands looming over the sofa.*

Linda   Here you go.

Stew *kisses* **Linda** *passionately, and* **Linda** *responds passionately.* **Stew** *puts his hands up her T-shirt, and she attacks his jean belt.* **Mrs Snowball** *and* **Seth** *are open mouthed.*

Mrs Snowball   Mister Bradwell!

Bradwell *springs up from the armchair and shows himself.*

Bradwell   Come out of character!

Linda *and* **Stew** *separate. Laughing. They both stand and wander about, shaking out their arms, loosening up, but both still laughing.* **Stew** *breaks up a chair and puts a couple of the loose legs on the fire.*

Mrs Snowball   Mister Bradwell?! What were going off over there? I don't put up with monkey business in my houses. I'm a respectable landlady!

Bradwell   Linda and Stew are actors. You've met Linda, Stew arrived from Manchester yesterday. They were improvising a scene. Theatre.

Mrs Snowball   Him, over there, was tryna cop off with her, over there, and you, over there, was just watching them?!

Bradwell   I'm chuffed, actually, that you thought it was real. I thought you were traducing me, but your analysis legitimises my methodology, and any endorsement, from the layman is always gratifying.

Mrs Snowball   I'm not a layman.

Bradwell   Lay-lady.

Linda   Hello, our Seth.

Seth   Hello, Linda.

Linda   What happened to your dog?

Seth It had a shit, and then died. Have you gorra boyfriend?

Mrs Snowball You! Over there! I don't want the likes of you, actresses, talking to our Seth.

Mrs Snowball *points out the open fire.*

Mister Bradwell? What's this?

Bradwell That's the heat source for the rehearsal room.

Stew Mandatory Equity temperature is nineteen degrees centigrade.

Mrs Snowball You, over there! Were I talking to you?

Stew Sorry, Mrs Snowball.

Mrs Snowball What's this?

Linda This chair is a found item, in Coltman Street.

Bradwell Not yours. From a skip. The fan heater packed up.

Mrs Snowball I've had a fire before. Near lost the house. Silly buggers. She was Norwegian, and he was from Goole. Both lesbians.

Linda *He* was a lesbian?

Mrs Snowball Folk from Goole, they live like animals.

Bradwell What is it you want, Mrs Snowball?

Mrs Snowball The rent.

Bradwell I've paid, in advance, six quid.

Mrs Snowball That first six pound yer give us was the deposit on the furniture. You, over there! Giss that fan heater.

Stew *picks up the fan heater, and gives it to* **Mrs Snowball**.

Mrs Snowball (*to* **Stew**) You, over there. Turn it on.

Linda *flicks the switch.* **Mrs Snowball** *turns the switch on the device on. Nothing. She turns the switch on and off. Nothing.*

Mrs Snowball   You've busted it.

Bradwell   We used it for half an hour.

Mrs Snowball   On full, I bet?

Bradwell   Naively perhaps, we presumed it was safe to use it on the maximum setting.

Mrs Snowball   That's your deposit gone.

Bradwell   Argghhh!

Linda   It's freezing.

Mrs Snowball   If any of you was married you could keep each other warm. But none of you are, 'cause owt that's good enough for most folk int gonna be good enough for the likes of you.

Linda   Marriage is the institutionalised oppression of women.

Mrs Snowball   The trick with men, young lady, is separate bathrooms.

Bradwell   I told you we were a theatre company and would be living and rehearsing in the house. You did not tell me that there was a bloke from Sunderland living in the back room.

Mrs Snowball   What's wrong with Sunderland?

Bradwell   I have a verbal contract saying the *whole* house was ours.

Mrs Snowball   If he was from Middlesbrough I'd understand. Six pound.

Bradwell   I don't have the money at the moment.

Mrs Snowball   Them two, him, over there, and her, over there. They've got money. I sawed 'em.

Bradwell   No, no, no. That was acting. Reality, fantasy, fantasy, reality.

Stew   Monopoly money.

Bradwell   It's Tuesday, my Giro –

Mrs Snowball   – Mister Bradwell?! Are you signing on?

Bradwell   I am.

Mrs Snowball   You, over there, are you signing on?

Linda   Yes.

Mrs Snowball   You?

Stew   Me?

Mrs Snowball   Yes, you, over there!

Stew   I am available for work, yes.

Mrs Snowball   You told me you was a professional theatre company.

Bradwell   Mrs Snowball, let me explain how the arts are supported in this country. Basically, there are two sorts of theatre companies, those with grants from the Arts Council, like the Royal Shakespeare Company and the National Theatre, and then there are those directly funded by the Department of Social Security.

Mrs Snowball   Go on then. Entertain me.

Bradwell   Is this a test?

Mrs Snowball   Then, I might believe you is what you say you is.

Bradwell   Stew?

Stew   A song?

Bradwell   Please.

Stew *picks up the guitar and improvises a song. He strums a chord.*

Stew (*sings*)
    Fell in love with a fan heater
    Fell in love today
    Fell in love with a fan heater
    But it blew away
    Fell in love with a fan heater
    Better than chopping up wood
    Fell in love with a fan heater
    'Cause it looked so good.

Stew *stops.*

Mrs Snowball   Is that it?

Bradwell   No.

Mrs Snowball   There's more, is there?

Bradwell   Yes. Sing the rest of it.

Mrs Snowball   Him, over there –

Bradwell   – Stew?

Mrs Snowball   He can sing.

Stew (*sings*)
    It blew hot and cold and sundry
    But I didn't even care
    'Cause me and my fan heater
    We ain't going nowhere
    Fell in love with a fan heater
    Fell in love today
    Fell in love with a fan heater
    But it blew away.

Mrs Snowball   Fan heaters blow up, they don't blow away.

Stew   'Blew away' rhymes with 'Fell in love today'.

Mrs Snowball   And in't that just the problem with the arts.

Bradwell   What?

Mrs Snowball   You're more interested in what rhymes than telling the truth!

Bradwell   Concur.

Mrs Snowball   Don't know what that word means but I'll have my money in one hour or you're out, all of you! I'll have our Seth chuck yer stuff into street. It'll be shameful for you. Shame! That's a good word, if you can remember what it means! One hour!

She turns to go.

Our Seth!

Seth   I'm gonna bury the dog.

Mrs Snowball   Will you be alright on your tod, love?

Seth   I'm not on my tod. Am I?

Mrs Snowball   I'll not have you mixing with these sorts. Bury the dog, and then come home.

Linda   Was it a girl dog?

Seth   Dunno. How d'yer tell?

Mrs Snowball   Our Seth! Wash yer mouth out! (*To* **Bradwell**.) See! What you've done. Two minutes of mixing with theatre types and our Seth, my son, is talking dirty. I won't have 'Play for Today' on in my house. What I've seen of theatre it's nowt but drink, drugs, violence, sexual inter curse and gouging out pensioners' eyes.

She's gone.

Stew   Eh? Is there anything else, anyone else, buried in the garden?

Seth   All my pets. The ones wot died. Since I was thirty-seven.

Linda   Shall I put the kettle on?

Seth   If you think it'll go with your outfit.

Linda   Ha! That's funny, clever.

Seth   That's my favourite joke. I say that in our house, to me mam, every time she says 'I'll put the kettle on'. I must say that fifteen times a week. She always laughs.

Linda   I'll make you a cup of tea, love. I'll bring it out.

Stew   So we have a whole pet cemetery out the back, eh?

Seth   Aye. Tother side o' my rhubarb.

Linda   You grow rhubarb do you, Seth love?

Seth   I love rhubarb.

Stew   What's the secret with rhubarb?

Seth   'Oss shit.

Stew   Do you force it?

Seth   I have nowt to do with the 'oss shit.

Seth *leaves and heads to the back garden.*

Stew   You couldn't make it up, eh?

Bradwell   Making up the truth, that's what we do.

Linda   The scene?

Bradwell   The scene was brilliant, I loved it. It was desperate. Pathetic. Like people. Like hippies, like fuckwits. Like us. But it was ruined –

Stew   – by Mrs Snowball?

Bradwell   By one of your fucking stupid jokes. We don't do gags.

Stew   What gag?

Bradwell   Where can you get Lebanese red. Lebanon. It's a gag. Like where did you get that Dover Sole, Dover; where did you get that Chicken Kiev, Kiev.

Stew   Bakewell Tart?

Linda   Guildford!

Stew   Linda did a gag. *Breakfast of a boiled egg and a ciggy. That's unhealthy. What's wrong with eggs?*

Bradwell   It was truthful. A fuckwit might say that.

Stew   So Linda can have jokes, but I can't?

Linda   Oh, fuck off, Stew, grow up.

Stew   Mrs Snowball does jokes. *She was Norwegian, and he was from Goole. I think they were lesbians.*

Linda   That's just saying stupid things.

Stew   There are gags loose out there, in the real world, your real world.

Bradwell   You want to do gags, go and join the Royal Shakespeare Company.

Stew   Stratford-upon-Avon. Lovely. Japanese tourists. River Avon. Not the fucking Humber, is it. Shakespeare's birth place, it's not as photogenic as fish dock but . . . And, Stratford's a good place to be an actor because, unlike Hull, they've actually got a theatre.

Bradwell   Hull is the best place on earth to start an experimental theatre troupe.

Stew   Why?

Bradwell   Sign on in Stratford, there's a danger they'll find you a job!

Stew   I like Hull.

Linda   What do you like about it?

Stew   Polar Bear. Fish and chips fried in beef dripping. Blue and white buses, I'm Manchester City, aren't I. The women are scary.

Bradwell   Hull's perfect.

Linda   For us.

Stew   I'm on board, I am, you know, theatre revolution, but what's wrong with theatre anyway?

Linda   Oh no.

Bradwell   Most theatre is one long wank. If you want tragedy, go and watch Hull City. (*Beat.*) If you want comedy, go and watch Hull City. British theatre's had its head stuck up Shakespeare's arse for four hundred years. Why do all Shakespearean actors walk like they've shat themselves? I'll only ever go and see another Shakespeare if they promise to butt fuck Judi Dench. They should ban the bardy bastard. They only do him 'cause they don't have to pay royalties, because he's been dead for four hundred years!

Linda   He likes Chekhov.

Stew   Chekhov's dead.

Bradwell   He's not dead, they killed him.

Stew   Eh?

Bradwell   They murder him, every bitter sweet production they do. I would willingly chop down the *Cherry Orchard* and turn it to kindling –

Linda   – we need kindling.

Stew   Chekhov and Bo Diddley, that's what you told me when I joined.

Bradwell   I want theatre to be sweaty, exciting, unpredictable, like a rock gig.

Linda   The id let loose.

Stew   What's the id?

Linda   Freud. Lust, all the urges, you know.

Stew   That's called the id is it? I call it a boner.

Bradwell   Life! For fuck's sake, life! I'm not interested in *Lady Windermere's Fan*, I want to know about Lady Windermere's fadge.

Stew   Fadge? Sorry, I'm Manchester.

Linda   Fanny.

Stew   It's a good title, Lady Windermere's Fadge.

Bradwell   I'd like to do some old middle class bollocks like the *Winslow Boy* and then, at the end, when all the fat shiny bastards have had enough of clapping and laughing and they leave the theatre, there he is, England's future, the Winslow boy, hanging ten foot up, on a meat hook with his insides dripping on to the pavement.

Stew   We could do that.

Linda   I'm up for it.

Stew   Or we could replace Shakespeare with a song about a broken fan heater?

Bradwell   Yeah, it felt real. Well played, I like the song.

Stew   Thanks, man. You know, everyone told me you're a bit of a twat but I'm getting to understand you now, dig you.

Bradwell   Thanks, man.

Linda   There was a bit in the scene where it felt like nothing was happening.

Bradwell   Hull has a band called Nothineverhappens, it's the truth, because nothing ever happens, but life.

Linda   So the audience just sit there watching nothing?

Bradwell   If you go down Coltman Street, to number thirty-two.

Linda   Mrs Ascough?

Bradwell   Mrs Ascough, her new fancy man, and her three teenage daughters.

Stew   Three sisters. Chekhov.

Bradwell   Well played. If by some super power you could remove the outside wall, and by that same super power, you could sit on a seat where the wall used to be, and by that same super power you were invisible to the people inside the room, and by that same super power you could watch Mrs Ascough her new fancy man and the three teenage daughters do nothing.

Linda   I sit there and watch them and they couldn't see me?

Stew   Also known as peeping.

Bradwell   That's what theatre is, peeping!

Stew   What if there's nothing going on, in the Ascough's?

Bradwell   You'd be fascinated!

Linda   You could boil an egg with the sexual tension in that house.

Stew   Back to eggs.

Bradwell   The minutiae of life should be your obsession. Fascinate me before you try and make me laugh. And for God's sake, and this is the big problem with British theatre, please resist the temptation to entertain.

Stew   Less is more?

Bradwell   That's Hollywood. This is Hull.

Linda   *When in doubt, do nowt.*

Bradwell   Brilliant! That is brilliant, Linda.

Linda   Oh. Fancy that.

Stew   Mike, can I drop Astral, my character, the acid casualty? He's a cliché.

Linda   And he's too similar to India, me, they're both stoners.

Bradwell   Who else do you have?

Stew   I know a bloke, he's a journalist, local newspaper, Salford. He does funny voices all the time, sings songs from adverts, impressions –

Bradwell   – knows every line of Monty Python?

Stew   It's pathetic –

Bradwell   – truthful. What's his name?

Stew   Italian Dave.

Bradwell   He's Italian?

Stew   No, he likes pizza.

Linda   He's English?

Stew   He organised our footie team's Christmas AGM and ordered pizza for everyone. So we call him Italian Dave.

Bradwell   I'm fascinated by a bloke called Italian Dave who isn't Italian.

Stew   Haha! I've fascinated him!

Bradwell   Do it. But you'll have to do all the work again.

Linda   To fascinate, we need an audience.

Bradwell   I've written to every venue out there, the phone calls will start happening as soon as.

Stew   A telephone?! Very modern, very professional. Where is it?

Linda   It's –

Bradwell   – in a box.

Stew   It's still in the box it came in?

Linda   It's the phone box in the street!

Stew   Eh?

Bradwell   That white box with windows. Outside the door.

Stew   That's a phone box? I thought it was a small hospital.

Linda   The phone number we put on the marketing is the Coltman Street phone box number.

The phone rings.

Linda   Right on cue. The truth.

Bradwell *legs it out the room.*

Stew   He's a bit of a fascist, isn't he? Bradwell.

Linda   Iconoclast.

Bradwell (*on the phone*)   Mike Bradwell speaking,

Stew   Where's the dictionary?

Stew *finds a dictionary on a shelf and starts looking through it.*
Linda *picks up the guitar and picks aimlessly.*

Bradwell (*on the phone*)   . . . yes, we are offering bookings for our new show which we're rehearsing right now . . . it's difficult to say what it's about . . . it's improvised, devised . . . it doesn't have a title yet no . . . I'm not a wanker, you're a wanker, fuck off.

They've obviously put the phone down. **Bradwell** *sits on the kerb head in hands.*

Stew   I wasted half an hour yesterday trying to find the word camouflage in the dictionary.

Linda   It's not funny, Stew.

Stew   It is. I promise you. That is funny. Camouflage, blends in with all the other words.

Linda   I don't need it explaining!

Stew   Iconoclast, here it is between icing sugar and icterine warbler. Iconoclast – a twat who is a very long way up his own arse.

Linda   What's an icterine warbler?

Stew (*reading*)   'A songbird with bright yellow underpants.'

Linda   Underparts.

Puts down dictionary and aimlessly picks up the guitar.

Linda   An iconoclast is someone who challenges the orthodoxy or status quo.

Stew   Nothing wrong with Status Quo.

Starts strumming some basic boogie on the guitar.

Linda   Theatre needs challenging. I want to see people like me on stage.

Stew   Out of work actors?

Linda   I'm sick of kings and middle class 'anyone for tennis' types.

Stew   Where did you train?

Linda   I knew a fire eater who needed an assistant. I had a pair of fishnet tights.

Stew   Nice. Prefer stockings but . . . in our impros, I'm beginning to feel that Astral fancies India.

Linda   Yeah?

Stew   And that India, you know, fancies Astral. Little feelings. What about you, Linda? Any little feelings?

Linda   No. Just happy to be working with the great Stewart Bradshaw.

Linda *leaves,* **Stew** *strums on the guitar.*

Stew (*singing*)   That sexy fan heater, fan heater.

(*Spoken.*) Cheetah, litre, centimetre, repeater, peter, sweeper.

(*Singing.*)
   The fan heater, the fan heater,
   She left me for a bloke off Blue Peter
   With sold carpet sweepers

Enter **Bradwell**.

Bradwell   Alright?

Stew   Yeah, going well. Phone call? Have we got a gig?

Bradwell   Nope.

Stew   Linda's er –

Bradwell   – yeah?

Stew   She's, you know. Is she single?

Bradwell   She's got a boyfriend.

Stew   They always have.

Bradwell   Do you fancy her?

Stew   Yeah. Who's the boyfriend?

Bradwell   Farmer's son, from Doncaster.

Stew   I could have him killed. D'yer know any contract killers?

Bradwell   Are you working?

Stew   I will now go up to my room, and start getting inside the head of Italian Dave. He's a bit of a lad, he's a bit yeah, and a bit, woah, he's a bit get one in! Yeah. I'm gonna take the Mott the Hoople posters down and put some nudes up. Shit. I'll have to go out and get some porn. Grr, I hate buying porn, it's so embarrassing.

Enter **Linda**.

Stew   Hi.

Linda   Why are you saying hi, I was only in here five minutes ago?

Stew   Because . . . I am now Italian Dave and he's not yet met you.

Bradwell   Would Italian Dave be embarrassed buying porn?

Stew No. You're right. Dave finds it easy. Alright mate, yeah. I need a Razzle, a Mayfair, a Club International, gimme a Penthouse, and I'm gonna need a mansize box of Kleenex, yeah. I'm Italian Dave, and I don't give a fuck! Woah! Get in there!

He's gone.

Bradwell Stew fancies you. I told him you had a boyfriend.

Linda Do I have a boyfriend? Mike?

Bradwell Yes. You do.

Linda Are you sure? Are we alright?

Bradwell Why, what is it?

Linda You always want to investigate relationships that have gone stale. In the impros.

Bradwell I've got a lot on my plate.

Linda You should tell Stew, that you're my boyfriend.

Bradwell Na, let it fuck his head. Or you could tell him. Or are you enjoying the attention? He's just horny.

Linda Thanks. What's the letter?

Bradwell (*opening it*) From John Cleese. No cheque. Dear Mr Bradwell. Fuck off. Yours sincerely. John Cleese.

Linda Nice of him to write. Who was it? On the phone.

Bradwell Milton Keynes.

Linda And?

Bradwell We are not going to be playing Milton Keynes Arse Centre anytime soon. Didn't want to anyway. Fucking roundabouts.

Linda We haven't made love for two weeks.

Bradwell That's what it is, is it?

Linda   It's getting to you Mike. You don't have to do everything you know.

Bradwell   Oh, OK, good idea, I'll get someone else to make love to you then.

Linda   In most theatre companies the director is not responsible for putting the tours together, answering the phone, paying the rent, marketing –

Bradwell   – we're not selling Mars bars.

Linda   Yes we are.

Bradwell   Oh! Are we?

Linda   We're making a product. It needs a name. We need a name. If there isn't a word for it, it doesn't exist. We need to give the company a name, and the play needs a name.

Bradwell   We don't know what it's about yet!

Linda   It will be about people. About life.

Bradwell   Life. Would you buy a ticket?

Linda   Naked. We're all naked.

Bradwell   I'd like two tickets to see *Naked* please. Linda, that is really rather brilliant. Thank you. Well played. Come here.

They snog.

I'm sorry. It's not easy.

Linda   Share it more. And the company needs a name.

Bradwell   I know.

Linda   Something alliterative. Alliteration works.

Bradwell   The Ku Klux Klan.

Julian *enters. He is a smaller, delicate featured man sporting a dog collar. He covers this quickly with his hand as if he'd suddenly remembered the rules.* **Linda** *and* **Bradwell** *stop hugging.*

Linda You're a vicar? I saw the collar.

Bradwell Stop it. Rules! Linda, out!

Linda My song is ready. Whenever.

Bradwell Well played.

Linda *leaves.*

Bradwell You've been out with the dog collar on?

Julian I walked to town and back.

Bradwell And did Hull like you?

Julian (*acting*) I belong to a profession both energetic and nervous and the nature of my avocations since my ordainment have not prepared me for an hour in West Hull.

Bradwell What kind of reaction did you get to the dog collar?

Julian Hessle Road, pretty binary. The deckhands, the men, they cross the road when they see me, as if they've seen the devil. The women, on the other hand, flock. Took me an hour to get from the Half Way to Boyes.

Bradwell Boyesis. Don't ask why. It just is.

Julian One sallow, rather piratical man told me, with some pride, that West Hull is the second most pagan diocese in the United Kingdom.

Bradwell What's the first most pagan?

Julian East Hull. A woman, babe in arms, suckling, said she's not singing 'For Those in Peril on the Sea' ever again. It confers a false nobility on a nautical death, as if losing your life trying to catch one half of a fish and chip supper was some kind of noble sacrifice.

Bradwell And you replied?

Julian Jesus was a fisherman.

Bradwell   And she said?

Julian   'Norr off Iceland he weren't!'

Bradwell   They lost three trawlers a couple years back.

Julian   I promise you, I have been told. The main discovery, however, is that in Hull, all the pubs are open, and all the churches are closed.

Bradwell   Good work, well played. Come out of character.

Julian *makes a pop sound with finger and cheek.*

Julian   Michael, I'd like to write a sermon.

Bradwell   Write?

Julian   Yes, I know the patrician male intellectual sitting in his library, pipe smoking, writing plays is antithetical to your vision but –

Bradwell   – vicars are writers. Writing sermons is part of the job. It's what they do. So, it's in character. Do it.

Julian   What is it, pal?

Bradwell   I'm down to the bones of my arse. You got any bread? The rent.

Julian   About a quid. No food till Giro.

Enter **Seth** *with the spade in hand.* **Julian** *and* **Bradwell** *look at each other as if to agree to continue as* **Alex**, *the vicar.*

Bradwell (*sings*)   No food till Giro.

Julian/Bradwell (*sings*)   No! Food! Till Giro!

Seth   You a vicar?

Julian   Indeed, but I am not of a proselytising bent.

Seth   Would you bless the dog for us?

Julian   What kind of dog is it?

Seth   A dead un.

Julian   Certainly. A pleasure. (*To* **Bradwell**.) Coming?

Bradwell   Yeah, what a caper, let's give it a send off.

They all exit. Telephone rings and rings. A passer-by, a young woman, **Camo**, *dressed in a white boiler suit and orange Doc Martens, sporting a blonde wig, answers it.*

Camo (*on phone*) Hi . . . yeah . . . hang on . . . I'll go get him.

Camo *lets the phone hang down, and sets off casually to find* **Bradwell**. **Linda** *and* **Stew** *enter the main room.*

Linda   Must've finished. Kind of 'Interstellar Overdrive' or 'Silver Machine'.

Stew   Hawkwind?

Linda   Yeah. Just that constantly progressing pounding bass.

Stew *essays a pounding bass line.*

Linda   Yeah. Perfect.

Enter **Camo**. *She rocks to the music.* **Stew** *plays on for another bar.*

Linda   Camo? What is it?

Camo   Digging it.

Linda   This is Stew. He's new. New Stew. This is Camo.

Stew   We've just been talking about camouflage. Camo.

Linda   Camo as in Camilla.

Camo   First things first. I'm not Camilla, from today, I'm Slag, or the Slag.

Linda   You've changed your name?

Camo   Your name is just a unilateral action, a non-negotiable heavy trip laid on you by two unawakened old people, AKA your parents.

Stew   Slag or the Slag?

Camo   Yeah.

Linda   You've dyed your hair.

Camo   This is a wig.

Stew   It looks like a sex shop wig.

Camo   That's because it is a sex shop wig.

Linda   Well spotted.

Stew   I'm a bit of an expert on sex shop wigs.

Camo   I present as a slag, an objectified fantasy plaything, but when a man hits on me, I give the horny bastard both barrels of feminist theory thereby dialectically castrating the wanker.

Linda   Is it fulfilling?

Camo   I'm loving it. Someone on the phone for you.

Linda   Thanks. (*To* **Stew**.) Community.

Linda *legs it out to the phone box.*

Stew   What's your attitude, man?

Camo   I'm a living artwork. My life is my art, and my art is my life.

Stew   So I could buy you and hang you on the wall?

Camo   If you could afford it.

Linda   Hello! . . . yes, I'm Linda Bell, the business manager for the company . . .

Stew   Are you a prossie?

Camo   A prostitute?

Stew   Are you?

Linda   The show is called *Naked* . . . no there's no nudity . . . it's about the compromises that hippies make to put bread on the table.

Camo   Have you ever thought about what a man is purchasing when he pays twenty quid for a prostitute?

Stew   Er . . . a good time.

Camo   Absolutely not. Money is paid so that she leaves in the morning.

Stew   Oh yeah.

Linda   We have four more weeks' rehearsal . . . I'll get him to ring you . . . bye!

Linda *exits the phone box and heads back in.*

Stew   Money well spent.

Camo   His expenditure maintains the man's lack of commitment to a fulfilling, mutually beneficial supportive relationship.

Stew   That's quite enlightening.

Linda *re-enters and puts the kettle on.*

Camo   That's my job. Enlightenment through art.

Stew   What are you into? What turns you on?

Camo   Serial killers, mutilation, Nazi memorabilia, transgression, drugs, Charles Manson, you know, that kinda thing.

Stew   Do you want a cup of tea?

Camo   Ooh that'd be lovely, thank you.

Enter **Bradwell** *and* **Julian**, *still as vicar.*

Bradwell   Alright, Camo, got a new caper?

Camo   Yes, changed my name, I am now Slag.

Stew   Or the Slag.

Bradwell   You've always been a push over. Two lager and blacks.

Camo   Yes, but now I've taken it up professionally.

Bradwell   Camilla, Camo, is a professional weirdo. Unlucky, living round here, because she's constantly outclassed by the locals.

Camo   The bar just keeps getting higher.

Bradwell   I've seen that wig somewhere.

Camo   Paragon Street sex shop.

Stew   Gotcha!

Camo   I was given an Arts Council grant. Five hundred pounds.

Bradwell   What? You've got money?!

Camo   I've cashed the cheque and I shall burn it all outside the Polar Bear –

Bradwell   – no! No, no. Don't burn it. We have some drugs. You like drugs. We can sell you drugs. I've got some dough doughs.

Bradwell *empties his pockets on to the table. A pile of pills.*

Camo   There's a drug I've never heard of?

Bradwell   Caffeine, paracetamol and diclofenac. In one pill. Boost your energy, make your heart race, good chance of killing you.

Stew   You could mebbe get an Arts Council grant for that.

Bradwell   About ten there. Six quid?

Camo   They're Buzzers. I can get Buzz over the counter.

Bradwell   Cam! You've got five hundred quid, and we've got nowt!

Camo   Yes well, obviously the government wants to encourage me and discourage you.

Bradwell   What did they give you the money for?

Linda Walking around in a sex shop wig and raising the consciousness of Hull's sexist men about feminism.

Bradwell *trashes a fire-ready chair.*

Camo No, actually. The Arts Council thing is that I plan to marry my dog.

Stew It's all dogs, innit, Hull.

Julian Exogamy is a fascinating subject.

Camo And endogamy needs to be challenged.

Stew Excuse me!

Julian Endogamy, marrying within your species, exogamy marrying without.

Stew I'm not marrying without. What's the point?

Camo I challenge dogma. Accepted precepts. Marriage is the capitulation to sameness, but if you marry a dog that is unlikely to happen.

Stew The dog. What make is he?

Camo The dog's a she, a bitch.

Linda Because marrying a dog of the opposite sex would be too conventional.

Camo Predictable.

Julian Have you announced the banns?

Camo The banns?

Julian Announcing the banns gives the community an opportunity to raise any legal objections to the marriage. Has the dog been married before?

Stew Yeah, she might be a professional bigamist.

Camo Definitely not. She's a Yorkshire Terrier.

Julian But you've only got her word for that.

Camo   I see your point, Father. What do I have to do to announce the banns?

Julian   I can do that for you. But there is a charge of six pounds to cover the registration and publication.

Linda   You have to do it properly or you're not subverting conventions.

Camo   Alright. Voilà.

Camo *pays* **Julian** *six pounds.*

Julian   Thanks. I'll raise the paperwork. Come back tomorrow, with the dog.

Camo   Au revoir, à la prochaine!

Camo *leaves.*

Julian (*handing over the money*)   The rent.

Bradwell   Well played. Well played. Well played.

Linda   There was a phone call. The Gulbenkian. Can you ring them back?

Stew   What?! A booking?

Linda   I told them the play was called *Naked*. They're interested.

Bradwell   Linda, I love you.

Bradwell *kisses her.* **Stew** *watches.*

Stew   Yeah, well done, Linda.

Stew *kisses her too.* **Linda** *is not willing but still kissed.* **Bradwell** *is annoyed.*

To black or equivalent.

The Truck

Another day. **Julian** *is on drums.* **Bradwell** *on tambourine and synthesiser.* **Linda** *on electric guitar. They are looking at lyric sheets/music scores.*

Bradwell   Your Spotlight entry said you can do a Geordie accent and play the drums.

Julian (*Geordie*)   Way aye man, photocopier.

Bradwell   And play the drums?

Julian (*Geordie*)   I'm doin' my best, bonnie lad, and I'm keeping time.

Enter **Stew**. *He slings on his bass.*

Stew   Either I'm late or you're all early. Sorry!

Linda   One, two –

Stew   – hang on! Whose song are we doing? Mine. Are we doing mine? My song. Me. Me. Me.

Bradwell   Linda's song. Julian hasn't learned the drums yet.

Stew   You haven't learned the drum part of my song?

Linda   No. He hasn't learned the drums. One, two, three, four –

Stew *kicks in with the driving bass.* **Julian** *drives it further with the drums.* **Bradwell** *makes weird noises with the synthesiser. It's a proper full on rock song with a guitar solo.*

Linda (*sings*)
 The ocean has been poisoned
 The fish can't breathe
 The universe is dying
 Time to leave
 The temperature is rising
 Rising fast

The ice caps are all melting
Just can't last
The polar bears are crying
No more snow
The universe is dying
Time to go
The star ship is waiting
To carry us way past mars
We are the generation
To return to the stars
Whoa whoa whoa
Those we take will have minds like us
With fully expanded consciousness
All we need are the simple things
Like the tarot cards and the old i ching
Everyone knows you gotta go with the flow
So set your controls for the great unknown
With captain kirk as commander in chief
And scotty on the engines for some comic relief.

Guitar solo.

The star ship is waiting
To carry us way past Mars
We are the generation
To return to the stars

Ends.

Julian   Janis Joplin may be dead, but her spirit lives on.

Stew   All you have to do now is OD on smack.

Bradwell   Maybe we can put that song in the cabaret.

Stew   In the what?

Linda   We need to develop an hour's cabaret.

Julian   Why?

Bradwell   Money. We need money.

Linda   To buy a van.

Julian   Why do we need a van?

Bradwell   To get to the cabaret!

Linda   I spoke to Northern Foods. They might give us some money.

Bradwell   Or, give us an old bread van.

Stew   A van made out of bread? What if it rains?

Julian   Birds?

Linda   Graham Burke, marketing director for Yorkshire and Humberside, he's visiting, here, today. Four o'clock.

Bradwell   Can everyone try and not call him a capitalist pig.

Julian   We look like a bunch of freaks.

Stew   We are a bunch of freaks.

Bradwell   I'd love it if we could offer him a cup of tea.

Julian   What?! You mean actually start a new tea bag?

Bradwell   In a clean cup. And a biscuit.

Julian   Are you mad?! Where are we going to get a biscuit?

Bradwell   For fuck's sake!

Linda   I know it's a pain meeting a Tory but we need the bread, to buy a van, to get to gigs, to earn bread!

Bradwell   That is how capitalism's pointless merry-go-round works.

Stew   Are you Workers Revolutionary Party?

Bradwell   Fuck off.

Stew   Socialist Worker?

Bradwell   Fuck off.

Stew   Nazi party?

Bradwell   They had good costumes.

Linda   We're not trying to change the world.

Bradwell   People who are preachy, political, proselytising, they're only like that, because they're not getting a shag.

Stew   Gandhi?

Bradwell   Not getting a shag.

Stew   The Dalai Lama?

Bradwell   Not getting a shag.

Stew   Mike Bradwell.

Linda   Not getting a shag.

Bradwell   Every man's quotidian imperative, every minute of every day, and with everything he does, is driven by, will this reduce the amount of time before the next shag.

Linda   Is this true of you, Julian?

Julian   Male motivation is complex. A man, for example, doesn't put up a set of book shelves simply because the family home needs more storage space. There are credit points to be earned.

Bradwell   Might be a shag down the line.

Stew   Do the washing up.

Bradwell   Might be a shag, down the line.

Stew   Drive the wife's mother to the station.

Bradwell   Might be a shag, down the line.

Stew   Germaine Greer, do you agree with this?

Linda   You could build me a library, Stew, still wouldn't cop a feel.

Bradwell   Fascinate!

Linda   Graham has asked to see some of our work.

Bradwell   Can we do a scene between Italian Dave and India? Please.

Stew   I need shoes with chains on. Businessy shirts. And white socks.

Linda   He's not here till four.

Bradwell   Back to the cabaret, everyone –

Stew   – hang on. I signed up to be in a play, one play. Now I'm doing a play and a cabaret. You'll be having us doing a kids' show next.

Linda *and* **Bradwell** *look at each other knowingly.*

Julian   Oh no.

Linda   There's a lot of money in kids' shows across the school holidays.

Stew   It's got to be a gold rush.

Julian   So you plan to do a kids' show in the morning, a stage play in the evening, and after the stage play, a late night cabaret.

Bradwell   It's better than working for a living. For the cabaret –

Stew   – can I be the stand-up comedian?

(*Heavy Yorkshire.*) Evening, my name's Arthur Cock, I won't be long.

Linda   Not Arthur Cock!

Julian   Harry Scarborough, Billy Bridlington.

Stew   Clive Clacton-on-Sea.

Julian   Reg Cleethorpes.

Bradwell   Yes! Reg Cleethorpes! Well played.

Stew (*Northern accent*)   Bought the wife a jaguar for Christmas. Tore her to pieces.

Linda   No mother-in-law jokes.

Stew   I wouldn't say my mother-in-law is fat, because she's only eight stone four. She came with us on holiday, sharing a caravan in Filey for a week, and at no point did I consider killing her. On several occasions she encouraged me to drink more beer, saying that I worked hard for my family and deserved a restful holiday.

Bradwell *laughs.* **Linda** *puts her hands over her mouth.*

Bradwell   That is genius. Well played.

Julian   It's classic deconstruction. Jacques Derrida.

Bradwell   You've just invented a new form of comedy.

Stew   Can somebody write down what I said, when I said it, and why I said it, because I don't remember saying anything clever.

Knocking at the door.

Julian   Someone at the door.

Linda   Are we expecting anyone?

Bradwell   Beatrice.

Bradwell *exits.*

Stew   What do we know about Beatrice?

Linda   She's just finished Oxford.

Stew   It needed finishing. All that scaffolding everywhere.

Julian   Who said that? Italian Dave I hope.

Stew   Yes. I think. It's like a disease. Stupid jokes.

Enter **Bea** *followed by* **Bradwell** *who is carrying two suitcases.* **Bea** *is exotic. Perhaps a short fur coat, a cigarette, heels, a silk dress, or skirt, a beret, sunglasses.*

Stew   Phwoargh. Ding dong.

Linda   Hi! Linda.

Bea   Hi. Bea.

Bea *slips the fur coat off and hands it to* **Julian**.

Linda   I like your top.

Bea   Thanks.

Stew   I like your top and your bottom.

Linda   Stew!

Bea   I can't stay here.

Stew   No! That's not me, that's Italian Dave, my character.

Bradwell   Stew is struggling with the process.

Linda   'Italian Dave' is Stew's character.

Stew   My character drives a Ford Capri and is into pornography.

Bea   And you don't have a Ford Capri?

Stew   You got it.

Julian   Sharp.

Bradwell   I'll take these cases up. Show you the room.

Bea   Thank you, Michael.

Bea *exits the room*. **Bradwell** *follows*. **Linda** *watches, jealous*.

Stew (*to* **Linda**)   Mmm. 'Thank you, Michael.'

Linda   She plays keyboards and cello. Be useful.

Julian   Linda, remind me again, why are we putting on a cabaret?

Linda   To buy a van!

Stew   Truck.

Linda   Mike wants a van –

Stew   – truck.

Linda   – with our name on the side.

Julian   We don't have a name. Or a van.

Stew   Truck.

Linda   Why do you keep saying truck?

Stew   I don't like the word van. Sounds Dutch. Truck. Anglo-Saxon. Gritty. Tough.

Linda   Truck's American.

Julian   Truck is actually a truncation of truckle, a wheel or pulley, and is also the name of a cylindrical cheese.

Stew   My uncle might be able to get us a truck.

Julian   Who's your uncle?

Stew   The bloke who married my aunty.

Julian   Is he in the second-hand truck business?

Stew   Uncle Fin, he does cars up. And trucks. They're divorced now, him and Aunty May. Aunty May ran off with a trackside martial from St. Helens Speedway. He wiped a bit of grit from her eye, just like *Brief Encounter*. (*As* **Celia Johnson**.) 'I felt the touch of his hand on my shoulder for a moment, and then he walked away, away out of my life forever.'

Two years after that he divorced my Aunty May and married her sister.

Linda   Your mother?

Stew   No! Aunty May's other sister, Beryl.

Julian   But if he's working his way through your mother's sisters it's only a matter of time before he marries your mother and becomes your dad.

Enter **Bea**.

Julian   How's the room?

Stew   Single bed, isn't it? Beds and whisky, I always go for a large double.

Bea   The view, how can I describe what's happening.

Julian   The waste land, the paddock?

Bea   A short, bald man is masturbating a horse.

Julian   That's Pete, the rag and bone man.

Bea   Do you think he gets some kind of sick pleasure out of it?

Stew   He must do. Every time he sees Pete he runs to the gate.

Julian   Where did you train?

Bea   I've had no training.

Stew   Don't worry, we have a water closet. You just sit on it. You'll get the hang of it.

Julian   Stew, do you need to find some shoes, with chains on?

Stew   Yes. And shirts. And white socks. Sorry it's difficult.

Stew *leaves.*

Julian   What instrument do you play?

Bea   Piano.

Julian   Excellent!

Linda   Everyone has to write a song, explaining their character's motivation, state of mind, whatever. 'I used to be a hippy, I'm sick of drugs, I've got no money, got to make a living, I'm lonely, but I don't think I could take on another loser, I'm getting into God.'

Bea   That's brilliant. You're brilliant. I forgot . . . is there a shop nearby?

Julian   Joan's. Don't ask for butter, you'll get margarine. If you want butter, ask for best butter.

Linda   And don't ask her how she is.

Julian   She's just had a hysterectomy.

Linda   You won't get away for half an hour.

Julian   'Filleted me like a fish.'

Linda   'Turned the workshop into a playroom.'

Julian   You do know there's no wage?

Bea   Michael said I should sign on.

Julian   But you need to give them an occupation that isn't needed in Hull.

Bea   Award winning shepherd?

Linda   Perfect!

Enter **Bradwell**.

Bradwell (*to* **Bea**)   Are you OK to start work or do you –

Bea   – I guess I've got some catching up to do.

Bradwell (*to* **Julian** *and* **Linda**)   Go on then. Offski.

Julian *and* **Linda** *make to leave.*

Julian   Tomorrow, I thought I'd go up to Flamborough Head.

Bradwell   Good, chuck yourself off!

Julian   Bempton Cliffs is the only British mainland gannetry. They arrive in January and apart from the fulmar are the earliest breeding birds to return. Anyone interested? There's a train to Bridlington and then a bus. I thought it'd be fun if we all went.

Bea   I'd love to.

Linda   We'll all go.

Julian   Excellent. If only we had a van.

Linda   Truck –

Julian   – Hull Truck. Assonance. Internal rhyme.

Bradwell   I know what fucking assonance is you public school twat.

Linda   A name, for us.

Bradwell   Hull Truck.

Linda   Hull Truck.

Julian   Hull Truck

Bradwell   Sounds . . . hard. 'ull Truck. 'ull fucking Truck.

Linda   I like it.

Julian *and* **Linda** *leave.* **Bradwell** *breaks up a chair and puts one leg on the fire, leaving the chair standing on three legs only.*

Bea   Do we always start by burning the furniture?

Bradwell   You can go home anytime you like.

Bea   What's wrong with the fan heater?

Bradwell   It blew me away.

Kicks the fan heater gently.

Bradwell   Characters. I liked the shoplifter, drifter. Tell me about her again.

Bea   You choose in the end, yeah?

Bradwell   That's right. I know what the others are doing. So –

Bea   – you'll pick what you think might be –

Bradwell   – fascinating.

Stew *enters.*

Stew Have you seen what he's done? Out the back.
Our Seth.

Bradwell   Stew. We're –

Stew   – he's buried the dog, but he hasn't dug a big enough
hole. All four legs are sticking up.

Bradwell   We're working.

Stew   Sorry. The legs . . . like . . . furry plants.

Stew *leaves.*

Bea   The shoplifter I know, she's basically a runaway, she
bums around the country, making temporary friends,
sleeping on sofas. She steals everything, food, clothes, you
know, everything. Hitches between cities. She's looking for
kicks, stimulation and she doesn't mind if it's kinda negative.
Weird. Sleeps with anyone who can give her a meal, or a
drink. She wears big combat jackets, camouflage trousers,
boots. Confrontational, aggressive.

Bradwell   Dangerous caper. Why is she like that?

Bea   She had a baby when she was fifteen and they took it
off her.

Bradwell   She steals because they took her baby? Don't
believe it. Kinda shit a playwright would think up.

Bea   She kept a lock of her baby's hair in a clasp.

Bradwell   Give her a new name. Write a biography. Mother,
father, growing up, school. If I ask you what O levels she
achieved, you tell me right away, and the grades, and why, if
they're good or not good. Decorate your room like her,
clothes. Create her. Keep it real. Fascinate me.

Bea   But make it up?

Bradwell   That is what we're doing here. We're making up
the truth.

Bea   Great. So I go out, into Hull, as her, yeah?

Bradwell   Yeah. We need a new fan heater.

Bea   What?

Bradwell   Go and nick a fan heater.

Bea   But that's –

Bradwell   – shoplifting?

Bea   Oh man?!

Bradwell   Think yourself lucky, we're not doing *Richard the Third*.

Bea   I'd have to kill the kids in the Tower?

Bradwell   Exactly.

Bea   When's opening night?

Bradwell *avoids the question.*

Bea   We don't have any gigs, do we?

Bradwell   Not at the moment, no.

The phone rings in the street.

That might be one now.

Bradwell *leaves, passing* **Linda** *in the doorway.*

(*To* **Linda**.) I'll get it.

Bea *sits and puts her head in her hands. Enter* **Linda**.

Linda   You OK?

Bea   I'm not sure.

Linda   You can't tell me anything about your character.

Bea   Yeah, yeah. Jeez, tough though. Tough.

Bradwell (*on the phone*)   Mike Bradwell!

Linda   Yeah. You've got to do stuff sometimes that you, your real self, wouldn't ever do for moral reasons.

Bea   Yeah. I don't have to tell my father. He wanted me to be a professional musician.

Bradwell (*on the phone*)   It's a cabaret, variety show, turns, magic, mind reading, I eat my own brains.

Enter **Stew** *with three stripey businessman style shirts, creased.*

Stew   Hey, hi, hi Bea?

Bea   Hi.

Stew   Found some shirts. Charity shop. This one's got some buttons missing, and they all need a wash.

Bea   I buy all my clothes from charity shops and they're always clean.

Stew   And they need refreshing, and ironing.

Linda   Iron them then.

Stew   Me?

Linda   You.

Stew   Me and irons, we . . . it's a long story, we don't get on, a bad experience, I failed physics O level. I can draw a vacuum flask.

Linda   Sex role stereotyping.

Stew   I am good at that, what I can't do is iron. Come on. Please. Girls.

Linda   If you were in character, I might forgive you, but you're not, you're Stew and you're asking us to wash and iron your shirts.

Stew   Yeah! Please. And the answer is?

Bea   Go fuck yourself.

Stew   I'm not asking for a fuck, I only want some shirts ironed. What am I going to do? My mother lives in Manchester!

Stew *leaves.*

Bea   Are you Spare Rib or Women's Voice?

Linda   As in 'is the problem men or capitalism?'

Bea   That's the big dichotomy.

Linda   Big dickotomy.

Bradwell (*on the phone*)   Do we get a sound check? . . . A sound check?

Bea   He's into you, you know that, don't you?

Linda   You haven't been here five minutes.

Bea   The way he looks at you.

Linda   I'm in a relationship with Mike.

Bea   I didn't know that.

Linda   But for some reason, stupidity, probably, even though he lives here, Stew hasn't clocked it.

Bea   All men are trash.

Linda   You're single then?

Bea   Staying that way too. I had a guy, the last guy, hopeless.

Enter **Bradwell**, *unseen.*

Bea   I mean, most men wouldn't know what a clitoris was if it jumped up and bit them on the leg.

Linda   Ha!

Bradwell   All I heard was the word clitoris.

Linda   Keyhole Kate.

Bradwell   I was not listening at the keyhole. But yes, I am now –

Linda   – fascinated.

Bradwell   The play I would like to see is women talking about men. What do women really think about men?

Bea   You wouldn't want to see that play.

Bradwell   I would. Let's see if we can get that into *Naked*.

Enter **Julian**.

Julian   Who was that? On the phone?

Bradwell   We've got a gig. Cabaret. Hull Blind Institute.

Linda   The audience are blind?

Bradwell   The audience are not blind, the room belongs to the Hull Blind Institute.

Julian   Oh shit.

Linda   When?

Bradwell   Friday.

Linda   Next Friday?! As in this Friday?

Bradwell   We will be paid, cash, but there may not be a sound check.

Linda   How come no sound check?

Bradwell   I asked 'will there be a sound check' and she said 'no, we pay cash'.

Julian   We're doing Stew's song, yeah.

Enter **Stew**, *with bass and lyric sheets. He hands them out as he talks.*

Stew   Bea, can you read music?

Bea   Do bears shit in the woods?

Stew   I can't write music. I'm like any of the Beatles.

Bea   I can be like Billy Preston, and join in.

Stew   So for this song, think Rolling Stones meets George
Formby.

Bea   I can't get no satisfaction when I'm cleaning windows.

Stew   Julian!

Julian   One, two, three, four.

'Existential Crisis' – Italian Dave's song

(*Singing.*)
    They call me Italian Dave
    I don't know who I am
    My situation's really grave
    I don't know who I am

    All I care for's sex and booze
    I tell bad jokes to amuse
    I get distracted by bums and boobs
    White socks is what I choose
    I don't know who I am

    I'm living though an existential crisis
    I don't know what my life is
    It's so much worse than arthritis
    I don't know who I am!

    I'll get these love, it's my round
    I don't know who I am
    Do you like me fooling around
    I don't know who I am

    Drink up baby, let's get outa this bar
    We can fool around in the back of my car
    Can you help love, I can't do your bra
    My personality needs a sticking plaster
    I don't know who I am

    I'm living though an existential crisis
    I don't know what my life is
    It's so much worse than cystitis
    I don't know who I am!

I'm like a ship without much ballast
I don't know who I am
My life is ruled by my phallus
I don't know who I am.

Enter **Mrs Snowball**.

Mrs Snowball   You're still here then?

Bradwell   Don't knock, just let yourself in.

Mrs Snowball   You! Over there?

Bradwell   This is Bea, she's an actor. I have the rent, Mrs Snowball.

Mrs Snowball   You'd better have 'cause I'll go and gerr our Seth if not.

Bradwell *goes in his pockets.*

Mrs Snowball   You, over there. What kinda fur is that?

Bea   I honestly don't know, it's my great aunt's.

Mrs Snowball (*pointing out her own coat*)   Mink. Sixty-seven of the little bastards. Bought it mesen. No man coughed up for this.

Bea   In this cold, you should get some trousers made to match.

Mrs Snowball   Eh?! What she say?

Bea   Bye. I'm going out, in character, I may be some time.

Bradwell   The rent.

Bradwell *hands over the rent.* **Mrs Snowball** *takes the money.*

Mrs Snowball   Who's that? There, over there?

Bradwell   This is the very reverent Alex Bridie.

Mrs Snowball   A vicar?

Julian   I am indeed, the shepherd to your sheep.

Mrs Snowball   Cushy job, one day a week.

Julian   I'm extremely busy, Mrs Snowball. Christenings, weddings, funerals. Confirmation class, as well as manning the phones through the night for the Samaritans.

Mrs Snowball   The Samaritans?! I don't trust them. If they really cared, they'd ring you.

Julian   This week is Epiphany and I have about seventy meetings.

Mrs Snowball   What's Epiphany?

Julian   From the Greek, a light coming forth from within. As in the revelation of Jesus to the Gentiles. It's the same root as 'epistemology'.

Mrs Snowball   He pissed them all off. That's why they crucified him.

Bradwell   What are you having for the feast of Epiphany?

Julian   Haddock and chips and mushy peas.

Mrs Snowball   I go to Gainsborough.

Julian   The fish restaurant. I've heard it's marvellous.

Mrs Snowball   The toilets are beautiful.

Julian   You prefer to sit down, do you?

Mrs Snowball   I'm a woman, I bloody well have to!

Bradwell   He meant sit, to eat. Fish and chips.

Mrs Snowball   You can't sell God to me, young man. There's only so many times you can knock on a door and if it never opens you'd be daft to think there's anyone in.

Julian   Yet God has already sent you his only son.

Mrs Snowball   Our Seth is Jesus Christ?!

Julian   I'm not saying that your Seth –

Mrs Snowball   – our Seth!

Julian   Your Seth –

Mrs Snowball   – our Seth!

Julian   I'm not saying that our Seth is Jesus Christ.

Mrs Snowball   You want your head testing!

There is a knock at the door. **Bradwell** *looks at his watch.*

Bradwell   Four o'clock.

Linda   Northern Foods. I'll get it. He's mine.

Linda *leaves to let in* **Graham**.

Mrs Snowball   I seen a sign outside of St. Martin's yesterday, 'God helps those who helps themselves'. In my book, that's thieving.

Julian   That is the parable of the ten virgins.

Mrs Snowball   And good luck finding ten o' them round here.

Enter **Graham Burke** *with* **Linda** *following.*

Graham   Hello!

Linda   I'm Linda, the business manager, we spoke on the phone. This is Mike, our director.

Bradwell   Hi.

Graham *shakes hands in a corporate way.*

Linda   This is Julian, who's playing –

Julian   – Alex Bridie. Vicar of St. James the Less.

Hand shake.

Linda   And Mrs Snowball –

Graham   – haha! Great costume!

Mrs Snowball   You what?!

Bradwell   Mrs Snowball is our landlady. She's in a good mood, I've just paid the rent.

Graham *laughs. He offers her a card.*

Graham   Graham Burke, Northern Foods, would you like a card?

Mrs Snowball   What do I want a card fo'? It's not Christmas!

Linda   Sit down, Graham.

Graham *chooses a three legged chair off the firewood pile, which immediately collapses under him.*

Bradwell   No! Not that one.

Julian   That's for the fire.

Mrs Snowball   Now, that is proper comedy.

They fuss around him, find him a new chair, and **Julian** *chucks the old one on to the fire.*

Bradwell   Can we offer Graham a cup of tea?

Linda   How do you take it?

Graham   Hot and wet!

Linda *exits.*

Graham   Bit of an entrance!

Bradwell (*to* **Mrs Snowball**)   Northern Foods might sponsor us, the theatre company.

Mrs Snowball   Are you the lot what's taken over Hull Brewery?

Graham   Indeed. Northern Foods.

Mrs Snowball   You're the reason I can't gerr a pint of Mild no more.

Graham   We have discontinued Hull Brewery Mild, yes.

Mrs Snowball   'Cause?

Graham   The market research . . . we asked three thousand Hull residents, customers, and the results were clear, Mild is becoming less popular.

Mrs Snowball   Yer never asked me. I drink Mild in the pub, and at home Nut Brown.

Graham (*worried*)   The bottled brown?

Mrs Snowball   The one with the little brown squirrel on the label.

Graham   Right.

Mrs Snowball   Oh no. You an't gorr any plans for Nut Brown have yer?

Graham   Sales of Nut Brown are in decline with the younger market so –

Mrs Snowball *leaps to her feet.*

Mrs Snowball   – are you calling me old?!

Graham   No!

Mrs Snowball   You've gorra bloody nerve!

Mrs Snowball *grabs a chair leg and starts threatening* **Graham** *with it.*

Mrs Snowball   Are you keeping Nut Brown or not?!

Graham   The production of bottled Nut Brown ale is no longer economically viable. We are developing a lager –

Mrs Snowball   – lager?! Bloody lager! This in't Germany! Lager's piss!

She starts beating him with the chair leg.

You've ruined Hull you have!

Graham   Argh!

Julian   Mrs Snowball?!

Mrs Snowball   There weren't owt wrong with Hull
Brewery! I'll tell yer, for nowt! Money, that's all you're
interested in. You don't understand this city. There's folks
here that's all they got to look forward to, a pint of Mild, and
a bottle of Nut Brown at home. And you after gerrin' us all
drinking lager! This is Hull, we don't drink bloody lager!

Julian (*laughing*)   Mrs Snowball! Please!

Graham *is now on the ground and getting beaten by* **Mrs
Snowball** *and the chair leg. Enter* **Linda** *and* **Stew**. **Linda** *has tea
for* **Graham**. **Stew** *is in his Italian Dave costume.* **Bradwell** *is now
laughing helplessly but trying to hide if from* **Graham** *who is
cowering on the floor protecting his head.*

Stew   Alright, a rumble! Whose side are we on?!

Linda   Mrs Snowball! Stop it!

Linda *gives the tea to* **Stew** *then manages to grapple the chair leg
from* **Mrs Snowball**.

Mrs Snowball   That'll learn yer. And if you, at some point
in the future discontinue Hull Brewery Nut Brown, I'll
come and find you, you won't be able to sleep, I'll hunt you
down, I knows everyone, there's no hiding from Hermione
Snowball in Hull, Hessle and 'altemprice!

Mrs Snowball *kicks* **Graham** *and leaves.* **Bradwell** *helps*
Graham Burk *off the floor.*

Bradwell   Graham. Stew, can you get Mister Burke a glass
of water.

Stew   There's his tea here.

Gives him his tea.

Are you a berk? My character's a berk.

Bradwell (*shouting*)   Stew! This is Stewart, another actor.

Graham   Has she gone?

Bradwell   She's gone. We're devising a play –

Graham   – devising?

Bradwell   Improvising.

Linda   We're trying to get away from the concept of the middle class, privileged male, in his book-lined study writing about powerful people.

Graham   Why?

Linda   We want to see ourselves represented on stage.

Graham   Mad hippies.

Linda   Hippies yes, but also ordinary people like students, bakery workers, or, you know, the women in Humber Pickle.

Graham   We haven't bought Humber Pickle, that wasn't us, that was Fine Fare.

Bradwell   Graham, relax, she's gone. We aim to tour throughout Yorkshire and Lancashire. That's roughly your area for Northern Foods, yeah?

Graham   Yes.

Bradwell   In the scene we're going to show you, Stew's character, Italian Dave –

Stew   – I'm a bit woooo, bit wahey, get in there, get one in, do you want some, eh, eh, eh.

Graham   Right.

Bradwell   Linda's character –

Linda   – India –

Bradwell   – was a hippy in the sixties

Linda   – she fancies the vicar.

Bradwell   That's Julian.

Julian   I'm not in this scene.

Bradwell   The scene takes place in India's house.

Graham   Who's India?

Stew   Jesus.

Bradwell   Linda is the actress, India is her character.

Stew   Didn't you ever play doctors and nurses?

Bradwell   Stew. That's enough.

Graham   I've just been attacked by a psychopath in a fur coat.

Bradwell   Italian Dave is India's new lodger, and in this scene, they're both a bit tipsy, as they've spent the night in the Polar Bear.

The phone rings.

Julian   Hang on! Someone's phoning us!

Graham   That's the call box in the street.

Bradwell   Er . . . yes it is, yes. Ignore it Julian.

Julian   But . . .

Bradwell   Leave it! From the top!

Linda *and* **Stew** *mime coming in from the pub. The scene begins.*

Linda   Would you like a night cap?

Stew   To keep my head warm?

Linda   Are you like this all day? It must be exhausting.

Stew   Like what?

Linda   Trying to be funny.

Stew   Banter innit. Helps you get through the day. We had this bloke ring up this morning, he said 'I've been reading your paper for fifty years'. I said 'you must be a slow reader, most people can get through it in twenty minutes.'

Julian *appears and answers the phone.*

Stew There's this thick bird at work –

Linda – bird? You mean a woman?

Stew A girl.

Linda What makes you think she's thick? She might not have had the privilege of an education.

Stew She thinks Sheffield Wednesday is a public holiday.

Graham *laughs.*

Stew Cunni lingus is an Irish airline.

Graham *laughs.*

Stew Sherlock Holmes, a block of flats.

Graham *laughs.*

Stew Muffin the Mule, a sexual offence.

Graham *laughs.*

Linda Some people do have sex with animals, it's called zoophilia.

Stew Crocodiles. Not tonight, no thanks, I've got a headache.

Julian *returns.*

Stew Don't you hippies ever laugh?

Linda I was a hippy. Not any more. But I was there.

Stew California?

Linda The '60s. But I need some bread now.

Stew Hippy capitalist, they're the worst.

Stew *goes for a kiss.* **Linda** *pushes him off.*

Linda Do you think because you're renting a room in my house that you've got a chance of getting off with me?

Stew You invited me to the pub!

Linda So if a woman invites a man to a pub, that means she'll sleep with him, does it?

Stew Usually, yes.

Linda You need to do some work on yourself.

Stew I work on myself every night.

Linda Oh God, what have I done? I've rented a room to Benny Hill.

Loud banging on the door.

Julian I'll go.

Julian *leaves.*

Bradwell Keep going.

Linda You're not my type.

Stew What is your type of man?

Linda Beyond Neandertal. Hopefully Holocene. Hell will freeze over, defrost and freeze again before you get to snog me.

Stew *puts a cushion or something over his hard on.*

Graham Oh my God.

Linda You're kidding me.

Stew Keep shouting at me and it'll go down.

The door opens and a uniformed police officer enters, followed by **Julian**.

Policeman Sorry to interrupt.

Bradwell What's happened?

Policeman Does a Miss Beatriz Hotty, Hoti reside here?

Bradwell Yes, she's one of my acting company.

Policeman Mister Bradwell?

Bradwell   Hello.

Policeman   In her statement Miss Hoti says that you encouraged her to go shoplifting for a fan heater. Is that the case?

Bradwell   Her character is a thief, a shoplifter, and so –

Policeman   – *yes*, or *no*, would suffice.

Bradwell   I guess, yes.

Policeman   I am arresting you for conspiracy to take another person's fan heater without that person's permission or consent and with the intention of depriving the rightful owner of it. Would you accompany me to the station please sir?

Bradwell   Yeah. Yeah, no problem. Alright. Er . . . Graham. Mister Burke? Do you think Northern Foods will be interested in sponsoring us?

Pause, as he dabs his wound.

Graham   I think I'm bleeding.

To black.

Interval.

The Cabaret

A theatre curtain hides 71 Coltman Street. Microphones are set on cabaret stands front stage. The drums and bass and keyboards are front cloth, set to stage right.

Enter **Julian**, *on drums, he drums, solo, it's pretty good, he gets carried away, it's crazy, it's Animal, ends with a roll.* **Stew** *joins him on bass guitar/guitar. Enter* **Bradwell** *as a stand-up comedian/ compère.*

Bradwell   Hello, Prestatyn! You can do better than that. Hello, Prestatyn! What a lot of warm taffs. My name's Cuddley Dudley. Hello, Cuddly Dudley! You do that bit!

Audience   Hello, Cuddly Dudley!

Bradwell   Big round of applause for the San Masarello Trio! I said the word trio, and you looked at the band and there's only two of them, and you laughed. I didn't have to say bum or tits, or describe how yesterday I accidentally got my testicles trapped in a food mixer.

You should have bingo cards on your seats, maybe a pencil, stolen from the local William Hill's. It's a socialist bingo. So the first prize is a long weekend in North Korea; second prize is two weeks in North Korea. We'll play that later but first please welcome to the stage Professor Bromovsky from the Opium University of Leipzig . . .

The band kick into playing 'Mule Train' and **Julian** *takes the stage dressed in a dinner jacket and bow tie. The act is a straight rip off of the Bob Blackman 'Mule Train' with tin tray percussion.*

Bradwell   Thank you, Professor! I'm joined now by the lovely Grace Notes –

Enter **Linda** *and* **Bea** *in matching costumes.*

Together   Hello, Cuddly Dudley!

Bradwell   Hello the Grace Notes. Now you're going to sing a song for us after bingo, is that right? What are you going to sing for us tonight?

Together   'You Can't Go Back To Constantinople.'

Bradwell   It's called Istanbul now, isn't it?

Bea   That's nobody's business but the Turks.

Bradwell   I find the Turks delightful.

Linda   We've got our balls in a bag.

Bradwell   So have I. Oh, bingo balls. Are you ready, eyes down for a full house of socialist bingo. Come on, love, get your bingo card out. Have you got a pen? Do you know where you are? She's brought her dobber with her. And the first number is –

Linda   – Siamese twins, two of everything, but only one liver, the number 1.

Bradwell   The number 1.

Linda   Sodomy with a duck – 29.

Bradwell   The number 29.

Bea   Ghandi's breakfast – number 80.

Bradwell   Ate nothing. Gandhi.

Linda   Alcoholics Anonymous, on the wagon, the number 12.

Bradwell   Twelve-step programme.

Bea   Financially embarrassed Spanish beggar. Por four four, the number 44.

Bradwell   Number 44.

Bea   If the devil is six then God is seven, the number 7.

Bradwell   The number 7.

Linda   Elizabeth Taylor, married again, the number 8.

Bradwell   Married eight times to seven different men, Richard Burton twice.

Bea   World record for divine resurrection, three days, the number 3.

Bradwell   Jesus Christ, no one else even comes close.

Linda   Rock and roll death, two and seven, 27.

Bradwell   Jimi Hendrix, Brian Jones, Janis Joplin, Jim Morrison all popped their pills and their clogs at twenty-seven.

Linda   Sexual intercourse began in, six and three, 63.

Bradwell   Which was rather late for me.

Together (*singing*)   Between the Chatterley ban, and the Beatles' first LP.

Bea   They think it's all over!

Bradwell   All together!

All   It is now!

Bradwell   66.

Bea   Don't look at the view.

Bradwell   The number 69.

Linda   Judas, the price of betrayal, number 30.

Bradwell   Thirty pieces of silver, Judas Escarriat. The number 30.

Bea   Hungarian revolution, 56.

Bradwell   Educational bingo.

All   House!

Bradwell   There it is, ladies and gentlemen, socialism, equality in action, you've all won, you're all off to North

Korea for a very long weekend sharing the square route of fuck all. Now ladies and gentlemen, the Grace Notes with 'You Can't Go Back To Constantinople'.

Together (*singing*)   'You Can't Go Back To Constantinople.'

Bradwell   Big hand there for the San Masarello Trio and the Grace Notes. I'd like to say how beautiful the Grace Notes are, but that would be to objectify the female form, so I won't. Yes, I'm a new man, well you have to be nowadays or you'd never get your leg over. Now please welcome to the stage, a man who knows about sexism, Lonesome Tex Fetlock, the Yodelling Cowboy!

Stew *takes the stage dressed as a cowboy, with guitar.*

Stew   Howdy y'all? It's a pleasure to be here at the Blind Institute in Kingstown upon the river Hull. What a great city ya'll got here, it'll be beautiful when it's finished. Pretty murky that river, I betcha the catfish are swimming around in there wiping their eyes. I mean, what the hell did you Hull folk do with all the hills? You beat 'em all till they were flat? Respect, I ain't gonna fuck with you folk.

This is a little song I wrote for my lying cheating wife. She wasn't much to look at but she looked pretty good through the bottom of a glass. We had two kids, and she's the reason they're both ugly. But she's left me now, and to be honest, I'm so miserable, it's just like having her home.

But I still love her, because her worst, was the best I'd ever had.

(*Singing.*)
>   I know you're leaving me tomorrow
>   For another cowboy, his name is Jim
>   What does he do, that I don't do?
>   'Cause I can learn to do the same
>
>   Does he rope and throw you like a steer?
>   Does he talk French in your ear?
>   Does he cook and clean and shower?
>   Does he love you every hour?

How can I get closure over you babe
When you're opening for him?
You sucked the wind right out my sails babe
But it's blowing hard for Jim

Does he rope and throw you like a steer?
Does he wear an ear ring in his ear?
Does he bake with whole grain flour?
Does he use words like empower?

I won't miss your style of cooking
I can burn shit on my own
Don't take my dog when you are leaving
She at least appreciates a bone

Does he rope and throw you like a steer?
Does he talk French in your ear?
Does he cook and clean and shower?
Does he love you every hour?

Yodellay, yodella *etc. yodelling.*

Bradwell   Lonesome Tex Fetlock there. Feeling a bit
peckish, madam, lady there in the third row back, yes, you
madam, you're wearing a daffodil? Would you mind, thank
you.

He eats it.

Smashing. Next we have the great mind reading act,
Gypsyville Claire Voyant!

Enter **Bea**, *dressed as a clairvoyant.*

Bea   Good evening, Cuddly Dudley.

Bradwell   You're not in a trance yet, Claire.

Bea   No, but –

She suddenly violently goes into a comedy trance.

Bradwell   Are you –

Bea   – I'm getting something!

Bradwell   Lucky you, I'm not getting anything.

Bea   There's a man –

Bradwell   – there's a man here!

Bea   – or possibly a woman, here tonight, in row . . . K –

Bradwell   – row K!

Bea   – seat number twenty-four.

Bradwell   Row K seat number twenty-four?! That's you, madam. Stay there, Equity members only on stage.

Bea   First madam, for the audience, have I ever met you before?

Audience   No, never.

Bradwell   Speak up please love, you've got to hit the back row.

Audience   No, never!

Bradwell   Calm down, love.

Bea   Has anyone from this theatre approached you and asked you to provide any personal information?

Audience   Only when I was buying the tickets.

Bea   Very good. First question. Have you ever walked past a shop?

Audience   Yes.

Bradwell   Brilliant! Round of applause, ladies and gentlemen.

Bea   And you live in . . . kangaroo.

Audience   No.

Bea   Wallerby?

Audience   Willerby.

Bradwell   Willerby! Amazing!

Bea   And your name, I'm getting, Santa, Santa Claus?

Audience   No.

Bea   Samantha?

Audience   Yes.

Bradwell   Amazing!

Bea   And your husband's name is, Leff, Heff, Geoff, Geoffrey!

Audience   No.

Bea   Ian? Is it Ian?

Audience   No.

Bea   John, Sam, Colin, Arthur, David, Tom, Gary, Peter, Philip.

Audience   Yes. Philip.

Bradwell   Philip. Round of applause, ladies and gentlemen.

Bea   And your husband isn't here tonight, is he?

Audience   No.

Bea   Do you know where he is?

Audience   I don't care where he is.

Bea   And children. I'm getting . . . nine children?!

Audience   I don't have any children.

Bea   Yes, madam, but I'm looking into the future.

Bradwell   Nine children in the future! Round of applause!

Bea   Do you have your debit card there?

Audience   Yes.

She gets it out.

Bea   Is it a Visa card issued by Nat West?

Audience   Yes.

Bea   And the long number does it start with 4821?

Audience   No.

Bea   4721?

Audience   Yes.

Bea   4721 3002 2155 2889 expires on –

Bradwell   – thank you, Clairvoyant! Round of applause, please! And a big thank you to Samantha! We'd like to end our cabaret this evening with a little sing along with the San Massarello Trio, the Grace Notes and Lonesome Tex Fetlock. Bit of Latin, 'Que Sera Sera'.

They sing 'Que Sera Sera'.

End cabaret.

Improvisations

The main Coltman Street room. Open on **Linda**, **Bea**, *and* **Bradwell**. *It's freezing cold again and* **Bradwell** *is trying to get the fire going, holding a double sheet of newspaper over the fireguard. Enter* **Stew**.

Stew   In the Polar Bear last night he said he wants us to work on a kids' show. Now, I became an actor mainly because I thought it would be easier than working for a living. But he wants me do a grown up's play, a kids' show, and then a cabaret all in the same day. I might as well get a job down pit, at least I'd get the evenings off.

Bea   A kids' show?

Bradwell   We have to pay the rent. I have said this before, it is my song, I do not have this week's rent.

Linda (*singing/improvising*)   We do not have the rent!

Bea   I need to talk to my agent.

Bradwell   Where's Julian?

Bea   He went to Spurn Point yesterday, bird watching.

Bradwell *kicks something, or chucks something across the room.*

Bradwell   Can't start without him.

Linda   We can do the news.

Bradwell   You do the news, you earned it.

Linda   We have a booking.

Stew   For what? Kids' show, cabaret, or the play?

Linda   The play. Hull University.

Bea   First night?

Linda   February twenty-third.

Bea   Two weeks!

Stew   Oh fuck.

Bea   What's the play called?

Bradwell   *Naked*.

Linda   Because we're all naked underneath.

Stew   I'm not naked. I'm wearing my lucky underpants.

Bea   Naked? No way, not in Hull in February. It's freezing.

Enter **Julian***, with a* Racing Post *in his hand.*

Julian   Sorry, mea culpa. Am I late?

Bradwell   Cunt!

Julian   I apologise. Theatre collective, all in this together, mea culpa. I thought you said ten, I presumed it was ten. I've never heard of a theatre company beginning work at nine in the morning. And, on behalf of the women, I object to being called a 'cunt'. The use of that word to defame is offensive and misogynist.

Bea   Thank you.

Julian   The female vagina is perfect.

Stew   Whereas the male vagina is a mess. (*Beat.*) Sorry.

Julian   A thing of beauty, like a lotus blossom. You wouldn't call someone you despise a lotus blossom. Would you?

Bea *claps.*

Stew   Vicar, we've got a gig.

Julian   Excellent. Bravo! When is it?

Bea   Two weeks' time.

Julian   Bugger me!

Stew   That might happen 'cause we're all gonna be naked.

Julian   Bit Germanic.

Bradwell   Where the fuck have you been?

Julian   I went to buy a *Sporting Life*, there's a National Hunt meeting at Sandown Park today. I don't like betting on the jumps, it's a ruddy lottery, but it's winter so what do you do. And then this biker gang, Hell's Angels, and yet all homosexual, I think –

Bea   – homosexual gang of homosexual Hell's Angels?

Linda   The Speedway House gang.

Stew   How did Hull get like this?

Bea   Did they beat you up?

Stew   Or bugger you?

Bradwell *looks around for a chair to break up.*

Julian   They asked, politely, to read my *Sporting Life*, and they wanted to know what I was doing in Hull, so I told them I was an actor, and they said they loved the theatre and would bring some fish round.

Bea   I don't get this city.

Julian   Presumably they've got access to some knock off fish.

Linda   Everyone in Hull has access to knock off fish.

Bradwell *smashes a chair up theatrically, dramatically.*

Julian   I'm sorry I'm late.

Bradwell *starts loading the fire with the chair.*

Julian   Wait! Stop!

Julian *wrestles with the chair that* **Bradwell** *is smashing up. It looks like* **Bradwell** *could kill him with a leg of it he's separated.*

Julian   This is a Mouseman chair!

Bradwell   What?!

Julian This chair is made by the Mouse Man!

Bradwell I'm gonna kill you!

Julian Peter Thompson. The Mouse Man. He's a furniture maker, works in oak and every item he makes has carved in it a mouse, somewhere. Look, there.

Bradwell *raises his arm aggressively.*

Linda Mike?!

Stew Don't kill him!

Julian I apologise, I just know a lot about everything. I'm sorry, that must be really annoying. But, to be honest, I like to share my knowledge because knowledge makes me happy, and I think it might make others happy.

Bradwell *throws the leg of the chair away and sits down.*

Bradwell We have four characters. Italian Dave, the vicar Alex Bridie, India the hippy –

Linda – ex hippy.

Bradwell – and the shoplifter, Moss. Julian, sit down!

Julian I'm sorry. I'm here now.

Stew Moss. What's the plural of moss? Mosses.

Julian It's the same as fish.

Stew The plural of moss is fishes?

Julian The plural of fish is fish, if it's a number of fish of the same kind, but fishes if you're talking about a number of different species. So you would say 'the fish are in the hold' if the fish that's in the hold is of the same species, but 'the Atlantic has over a thousand varieties of fishes –.'

Bradwell *grabs him by the throat and starts to throttle him violently. They all join in to stop* **Julian** *being killed, basically pulling* **Bradwell** *off him.*

Julian   Please forgive me. Let us make a play.

Bradwell *sits, slings his arm around his neck and grabs his chin.*

Bradwell   Bea, I sent you, as Moss to the Paragon Hotel, yesterday lunchtime. Stew, you were sent to try and get off with her. How did it go?

Bea   I got the bus into town, didn't pay the fare. I nicked a Marathon bar from a newsagents, and flirted with the barman, which earned me a free pint of Guinness, but dangerous, I think he fell in love with me.

Bradwell   Citizens are collateral damage in this process.

Bea   Italian Dave came into the pub and rescued me.

Stew   Alright gorgeous?!

Bea   He paid for the Guinness.

Bradwell   Was there an attraction?

Julian   Did you sleep together?

Bea   What are you asking?

Julian   Sorry, are we allowed to ask that? I do not think it is possible to improvise a fuck.

Stew   Every fuck I've ever had has been improvised.

Bradwell   In fact, know-it-all, I do have a method of improvising a fuck.

Linda   Wait. I'm sorry. We need to know if you're sleeping together.

Bradwell   This is an exercise I nicked off Lee Strasberg.

Bradwell *moves the table,* **Julian** *helps.*

Stew   You want us to fuck on the table!

Bradwell   Put your hands on the table. Your hands are your bodies.

Stew   Always up for a hand job.

Bradwell   Sit opposite each other.

Bea *and* **Stew** *sit opposite each other and put their hands on the table.*

Stew   I hope you're on the pill because I don't have ten condoms.

Bradwell   Your hands are your bodies. It's midnight, you're both tipsy, you're back at Italian Dave's porn hell bed sit. Do it or don't do it.

Their hands are on the table. No one makes a move. **Julian** *laughs. Then* **Stew***'s hands make a tentative slow move towards* **Bea***'s hands,* **Bea***'s hands retreat, coyly,* **Stew** *slowly chases,* **Bea** *retreats, then gets cornered,* **Stew** *touches* **Bea***'s hands and* **Bea** *touches back,* **Stew** *uses a finger to stroke a finger of* **Bea***'s,* **Bea** *flicks with a finger causing an Ouch! from* **Stew***.* **Stew** *advances again,* **Bea** *accommodates,* **Stew** *climbs on top of* **Bea***'s hands,* **Bea** *flips him over and fucks him from on top.* **Linda** *claps at this,* **Julian** *laughs.*

Bradwell   So you fucked him?

Bea   That is part of Moss's game. She's getting free drinks, a room, scampi and chips, and a bed for the night, but also sex, she needs sex, she doesn't need love. She is scared of love.

Linda   She couldn't love Italian Dave, he's an idiot.

Bea   It's quite feminist really, she's in control, she's ripping him off, and she'll be back on the road in the morning.

Bradwell   Stew?

Stew   Yeah, well, I mean Bea's hot, I mean Moss . . . is hot. She is, so, you know, I'm a bloke, Dave's a bloke, he'll take what he can get even if he knows that she has the power.

Bradwell   This is good. What about you two?

Julian   Wawne church, almost in the country, on the way to Meaux Abbey which is a really interesting –

Bradwell   – Julian –

Julian   – sorry, we arranged to meet, accidentally, in Wawne church.

Stew   You had a dog collar on in someone else's church?

Julian   Wawne church shares a vicar with Sutton and I'd checked, I knew he wasn't going to be there that day.

Stew   Brave man.

Linda   India's mother was buried in Wawne church graveyard, and so we met outside.

Julian   It was very moving actually.

Linda   I found Julian's vicar sensitive, and caring, and full of fascinating tid bits of knowledge.

Laughter.

Which, amazingly, I found really quite seductive. India has a vacuum in her life –

Stew   – a hoover. Sorry. Really sorry.

Linda   India has a vacuum in her life, a yearning for meaning, and she began to imagine the life of a vicar's wife.

Bea   Wow.

Bradwell   Julian?

Julian   It was really quite a powerful afternoon. We one hundred per cent stayed in character. Alex and India walked down the bank of the river Hull, which of course is tidal, and we saw some Eurasian coots and Alex explained to India the four types of webbed foot – palmate, semipalmate, totipalmate, and lobate –

Linda   – and I loved that. All that informed intelligence, and sensitivity.

They look to **Bradwell** *for direction. He seems to have none.*

Bea   Hands. On the table.

Bradwell   Why not?

Julian *and* **Linda** *sit opposite each other with hands on the table.*

Julian   Where are we?

Bradwell   You're in a bed and breakfast in Ravenscar. You've just finished the Lyke Wake Walk, so Alex has been talking bollocks non stop for sixty miles –

Julian   – forty miles. Sorry. It is forty miles, not sixty.

Stew   And Alex has knocked on your door because you accidentally left your Kendal Mint Cake in his underpants.

Bradwell   Yeah. Let's see it.

Julian *puts his hands on the table. He's wearing a shirt with the cuffs buttoned down.* **Linda** *puts her hands on the table. She has bare arms but rings and a watch on. It goes quiet. No one makes a move.* **Julian** *undoes his cuff buttons and rolls his sleeves up.* **Bea** *claps.* **Stew** *laughs.* **Bradwell** *does his habitual face grapple, he's tense.* **Linda** *takes off her watch and her rings.* **Bea** *claps,* **Stew** *laughs,* **Bradwell** *tightens his grapple grip. Both pairs of hands are now on the table.* **Linda** *slowly loosens her hands, relaxing the fingers so that they spread a little.* **Julian** *mirrors this.*

Bea   Oh my God!

Julian *makes a slight move forward with both hands.* **Linda** *mirrors this so that the tips of their middle fingers are touching.* **Bea** *is breathing hard. Both* **Linda** *and* **Julian** *noticeably relax in their seats and their legs touch under the table and they both lean back a little.* **Linda** *makes the next move, moving both her hands slowly and sensuously on top of* **Julian**'s *hands.* **Julian** *decisively releases a hand and uses it to remove* **Linda**'s *hands from on top of his and he puts his hands on top of hers.*

Stew   Quite right too.

Linda *takes the initiative and joins all four hands together in one ball.* **Julian** *rolls the ball one way, and* **Linda** *rolls it back.* **Linda** *lets her head fall back and eyes closed looks at the ceiling.* **Julian** *does much the same.* **Linda** *lets out an audible, low, satisfied groan.*

Bea   Yes! Yes! Yes!

There is a knock at the door.

Stew   Oh no!

Bea   I'll go. Who are we expecting?

Bradwell   The rent never sleeps.

Bea *is out the door.* **Linda** *stands and walks away to be on her own.*
Julian, *stands, maybe a hard on that he covers up. Enter* **Bea**
followed by a leather clad homosexual Hell's Angel carrying a tray of
frozen fish. **Bradwell**, *head in hands by now.*

Daz   There he is! Brought you that fish, lad. Wahey!

Julian   This is the biker homo . . . Hell's Angel fish chap I
was telling you about.

Daz   Daz.

All   Hi / Hiya Daz / Alright?

Daz (*Hull accent*)   I'll purr 'em own here by side o' fire,
they'll defrost while you're practicing yer play. Yer bonnin'
wood, eh?

Stew   Yes, we skip hunt.

Daz *picks up the Mouse Man chair, what's left of it.*

Daz   Wahey! Yer can't bon that, that's a Mouse Man chair.
Bit of quality erk is that.

Bea   Erk?

Daz   Aye, English erk. Wahey!

Linda   Oak.

Daz   Wahey! Yonder fish is mainly ducks.

Stew   Peking or . . .?

Daz   Haddocks! Wahey! You all actors then?

All   Yeah / Yes / Well . . .

Daz   What play are you learnin'?

Bea   We're making it up.

Daz   I've gorra story for yers, mek a good play. Wahey! Do you want to hear it?

Bradwell   Yes please.

Daz   I was having my coal nicked, and I worked out it's gorra be someone in tenfoot. I took a big bastard lump of nutty slack, wahey! drilled an 'ole in it, packed it full o' gunpowder from three big bangers. Filled the hole up with Polyfilla, painted it black and purr it back in my coal bunker. Three nights later, wahey! (*Mimes the explosion.*) Missus next door, who's forty-three, a widow, and on the game and obviously a thieving fucking toerag, comes screaming into tenfoot, dressed in nowt but high heels and the full flying kit with her client wi' a fast receding hard on. She's telling everyone that her fire's exploded and killed the cat, who, as it happens, used to piss on my lawn. It's got it all – sex, violence, justice, redemption and a social message. Don't nick my coal. (*Beat.*) That's a fucking play, innit?

Bradwell   Yes it is. It's brilliant. Thank you.

Daz   Tarra. We go to Flamingo's on a Friday. Come along. Girls welcome. And Julian love, like I said, you don't have to be a puff, just say you are. Wahey! Tarra!

He leaves.

Bea   What the fuck was that?

Linda   Welcome to Hull.

Julian   There's thirty quid's worth of frozen haddock here.

Bea   What are we going to do with it?

Bradwell (*standing*)   Linda, give Mrs Snowball a ring. Tell her we have a month's rent. We open a week Tuesday! All I have to do now –

Stew   – we. All we have to do now.

Bea   We're all in this together.

Julian   Adrift in a boat.

Bradwell   We . . . have to work out a way of getting these four very mad, very different characters meeting in the same room.

Bradwell *makes to leave. He gets to the door and turns.*

And Julian, I'm sorry I called you a cunt, you're not a cunt, you're a stupid fucking lotus blossom.

Bradwell *leaves in a strop.*

End of scene.

Repercussions

The main room. **Bea** *at the piano. It's night time.* **Bea** *sings her song.*

They took my child away
'Cause I was still a girl
They said I was a whore
I'm left with just one curl

They took away my scream
In the birthing ward
Screaming's for the pure
Pain is your reward

The church and state together
The Bonnie and Clyde of right
They thieve in the day
Taking in plain sight

They took my child away
In exchange a prayer
And everlasting shame
They left me with one hair

Forever incomplete
Outcast and depraved
A woman now turned thief
I shall have my day

To avenge you
My purpose every day
I'll claim and take and steal
And I will find a way . . . to you.

Enter **Bradwell**, *in Y-fronts with a fart hole in the back, carrying a sleeping bag.*

Bea   Mike?

Bradwell   That's me.

Bea   You're in here?

Bradwell   I am in here, yes. Where are you?

Bea   I'm . . . in here.

Bradwell   Are you sleeping in here?

Bea   No. I was working on my song.

Bradwell   Well played.

Bea   Did I wake you?

Bradwell   No.

Bea   Are you not sleeping with Linda?

Bradwell   Does it look like it?

Bea   Oh dear. You and Linda?

Bradwell   It's been coming.

Bea   I'm sorry.

Bradwell   Don't be. Love's a caper. Don't feel sorry for her. She's getting a good deal. She's getting shot of me.

Bea   Is it Julian?

Bradwell   No!

Bea   Have *you* met someone –

Bradwell   – no!

Bea   Do you want to talk about it?

Bradwell   No!!! I'm a bloke. I'll go drinking.

Bea   I thought I ought to tell you –

Bradwell   – yes?

Bea   Stew and I are sleeping together.

Bradwell   Good to know someone's getting a shag.

Bea   I was worried –

Bradwell   – I worked it out. I'm not stupid. And Stew bragged to me about it.

Bea   Bragged?

Bradwell   He knows he's punching above his weight with you.

Bea   Because?

Bradwell   You're gorgeous and from Oxford via Spain –

Bea   – Tunisia.

Bradwell   Tunisia, and he's an annoying little tosspot from Manchester.

Bea   We had this idea –

Bradwell   – just now, in bed?

Bea   Yes.

Bradwell   Did it work?

Bea   For the play. What if we all meet at one of the vicar's open house afternoons. Who is your house open to?

Bradwell   So Julian's shared his sermon with you has he?

Bea   Yes. Is he not supposed to?

Bradwell   No. Principles of improvisation. Little knowitall shit.

Bea   Linda would go, sorry, India would go, because she fancies the vicar, Italian Dave would go because he's close to a nervous breakdown –

Bradwell   – and Moss would go –

Bea   – because of what happened to her baby.

Bradwell   She blames the church?

Bea   She wants revenge. It's a deliberate plan to go to the church and steal.

Bradwell I like revenge. Dangerous.

Bea Yes, the baby. What do you think?

Bradwell I love it.

Bea You're crying.

Bradwell I do. Sometimes.

Bea When I was improvising that scene, with Stew, in the pub, where he was trying to pick me up, I noticed you, watching, taking notes, and then you stopped writing, and I saw you were crying.

Bradwell It's not illegal. Is it?

Bea Why were you crying?

Bradwell Do you have a problem with hairy-arsed blokes crying?

Bea You really feel, don't you? What set you off? A funny, made up scene in a pub?

Bradwell It was the need. On both sides. His need. Your need. The desperate human need. The failure to connect. The fear of saying what you really both need. It was too real. The chasm. The massive cock up that is humanity.

Bea Are you alright, Mike?

Bradwell I am. Thank you for caring. It's a great idea. You're a brilliant woman. Now turn the light off, and fuck off.

End of scene.

The Show

The set is **Alex**, *the vicar's house, within the Gulbenkian theatre at Hull University. The house lights are up as* **Mrs Snowball** *and Our* **Seth** *enter the auditorium looking for their seats walking up the rake.*

Mrs Snowball   Come on, our Seth!

Seth   I think we've gone too far uphill.

Mrs Snowball   What was we?

Seth   E. E for 'enry. E6. And he had six wives an' all.

Mrs Snowball (*to* **Bradwell**)   Mister Bradwell! What row are you?

Bradwell   F.

Seth   F?!

Bradwell   F.

Mrs Snowball   F?!

Bradwell   F!

Seth   F?!

Bradwell   F!

Seth   Don't you eff me?!

Bradwell   This is row F. What are you?

Mrs Snowball   E six and seven.

Bradwell   You're here then, in front of me.

Mrs Snowball   Excuse me, love. Yeah, leave your bag on the floor I'll enjoy treading on your compact.

House lights go down.

Sit down, our Seth. Can you see over his head?

Bradwell   He's not that big.

Mrs Snowball   Try giving birth to him.

House lights off.

Seth   Mam! It's gone dark! I need my blanket!

Bradwell   Shush!

Front curtain style, **Julian**, *as Alex Bridie addresses the audience. It's a sermon.*

Mrs Snowball   That's the posh lad, Julian.

Bradwell   Shush!

Julian   Who is your house open to? Who is your house open to? When I first came to Hull I went to the market in the old town and decided to go into Holy Trinity to pray – but the door was locked. So I went to St. Mary's, Lowgate, and that was locked too. So I tried St. Albans, St. Michael and All Angels, St. Bartholomew's, St. Botolph's – they were all bolted and barred. All of them, and when I arrived at this church, my own church, I couldn't even get to the doors because the gate at the end of the path was padlocked shut. I was told 'we have to keep the riff raff out.' Who is your house open to? As Christians, would you welcome the riff raff in here? Thieves, drunks, beggars, drug addicts, Muslims, Jews? Jews, where it all began? Jesus tells us the parable of the hundred sheep. He trusted the ninety-nine, and went after the hundredth, the lost one, the drunk sheep, the hooligan sheep, the riff raff. So it seems to me that most of the churches in Hull specifically bar their doors to the very people who God is most anxious to welcome in. Did you ever hear anything so bloody stupid? As Christians, we are missionaries and there are people out there today, during this week of Epiphany, on the streets of Hull dying of hypothermia, lost sheep, lost to drink or drugs, people living lonely and despairing lives who are just waiting for a hand to help them out of the rut. Who is your house open to?

Stage lights up on the set of the vicar's house with chairs around a coffee table. The table has sandwiches, cakes and a large pot of tea set. The teapot has a woollen cosy. **Julian** *sits and waits, looks at his watch. Feels the teapot, decides it's gone cold, and stands to put the kettle on. He is half way to the kitchen when Moss enters.*

Bea   I heard say you're having an open house? With sandwiches?

Julian   My door is open, yes.

Bea *walks in.*

Julian   Come in.

Bea   I'm in!

Julian *offers his hand to shake.* **Bea** *looks at it with contempt.*

Julian   Alex Bridie. I'm the vicar.

Bea   Do I look stupid?!

Julian   And your name?

Bea   Moss.

Julian   Are you homeless, Moss?

Bea   Home? Just another word for prison, innit.

Bea *sits and tucks into the sandwiches.*

Julian   There's egg and cress and –

Bea *picks out the bits of cress.*

Bea   – what is the point? Eh?

Julian   Of cress?

Bea   Of living. Fucking life.

Mrs Snowball   There's no need to swear!

Julian   Are you suicidal?

Bea   This tea's cold.

Julian   Oh woopse, I'll put the kettle on.

Seth   If you think it'll go with your outfit!

Bradwell   Shush!

Seth   I say that every time –

Bradwell   – I know, can you shut up, please?!

Julian *leaves the room for the kitchen. Moss takes the opportunity to case the joint. She is tempted by a huge glass jar, with a slot in the top for sixpences. It is three-quarters full of sixpences. Assesses how she can steal it but it's huge. She steals a couple of candlesticks, dispensing with the candles. Her flak jacket has very large pockets and deliberately stitched into the lining a shoplifter's pocket.*

Mrs Snowball   She's nicking stuff!

Julian *enters.*

Bradwell   That is the play, Mrs Snowball. Continue!

Bea *resets the candles.*

Mrs Snowball (*to whoever*)   If I see owt, I say summat. That's me.

Julian (*sotto*)   Are we resetting the candles?

Bea (*sotto*)   Done. Go from kettle.

Julian   I'll put the kettle on.

Seth   If you think it'll go with your outfit!

Julian *exits with the teapot. Moss takes the opportunity to case the joint. She is tempted by a huge glass jar, with a slot in the top for sixpences. It is three-quarters full of sixpences. Assesses how she can steal it but it's huge. She steals a couple of candlesticks, dispensing with the candles. There is a knock at the door.* **Julian** *enters, puts the fresh teapot down on the table, with cosy, and then crosses and opens the door. India is there with Italian Dave.*

Julian   India! What an absolute joy to see you!

India leans in for a kiss on the lips, but **Julian** *swerves and catches her on the cheek.*

Stew   What's this, Postman's Knock?

Linda   This is Dave, he's my new lodger.

Stew *grabs* **Julian***'s hand and shakes it in a forwards and backwards motion for too long.*

Stew   I used to work for British Rail. Ha, ha! Aye, aye there's another lost sheep here already. Dave or Italian Dave.

Moss just glares at him, says nothing.

Julian   Please everyone. Take a seat.

Linda   I found two sixpences for the new bells' fund.

She gives them to **Julian** *who puts two sixpences in the bottle.*

Julian   Smashing.

Linda   Must be nearly fifty pounds in there now.

Julian   Just another three thousand to go then!

Linda (*to Moss*)   Hello, I'm India.

Julian   This is Moss, she's . . . well, Moss can tell you herself.

Bea   I've come in here, 'cause he, the vicar, has a billboard out the front claiming to have all the answers.

Stew   I like a pub quiz.

Julian   There is an answer that works for almost every question, Jesus Christ.

Stew   Who won the FA cup in 1952?

Bea   Jesus Christ.

Julian Jesus is obviously not the literal answer to every question, but he is the light, a light that can be cast on all problems.

Bea Did he create the dinosaurs?

Linda Jesus was the son of God, not the creator.

Bea Why are you starting on me?

Linda I'm not.

Bea You don't know me, and yet you're having a go at me.

Linda I'm not.

Julian I am perfectly happy to answer the question did Jesus create dinosaurs. And I would say that the Lord God, did, yes.

Bea So you admit it, he fucked up.

To black / Lights up.

Stew I met some dinosaur birds in Middlesbrough.

Bea Shut it you. You are unbelievably annoying and misogynist.

Julian Moss, Italian David has come here, perhaps seeking a direction. That itself is brave and deserves admiration.

Stew I am, right now, seeking a bit of mustard.

To black / Lights up.

Linda What makes you so sure of everything anyway?

Bea I know the church. I know how they work. And don't worry about me, I'm not interested in him. You can have him.

Linda I don't know what makes you think I'm after the vicar –

Bea – girl! It's obvious, I'm surprised you haven't slipped off that chair.

Linda   Oh my God! That's disgusting.

Stew   I don't understand.

Bea   No, you wouldn't.

Stew   Why is that disgusting? Why would she slip off the chair if she fancies the vicar? Oooooohhh. I get it. Wow!

To black / Lights up.

Julian (*holding a jar of mustard*)   English mustard!

Stew   Colman's! Not the coalman's with an A, but Colman's without an A.

Bea   He also created mosquitos. Pure evol.

Linda   God is not a person. Not a he. God is everything. And in everything.

To black / Lights up.

Italian Dave is spreading mustard onto his sandwich. A lot of it. He looks at it. Decides to take a bite.

To black / Lights up.

Italian Dave takes the cosy from the teapot and puts it on his head.

Stew   This is cosy.

To black / Lights up.

Italian Dave is on his knees.

Stew   I'm . . . I'm sick of being like this.

Italian Dave puts his head in his hands.

Julian   The church is here to bring everyone together in love.

Stew   I'm a waste of space.

Linda   Dave. Love. It's alright. That's why we're here. Alex can help. I've seen him help other people. He has such a big heart.

Julian   Share it, David.

Stew   All day at work, I'm trying to make people laugh, drivel, drivel, drivel. I can't stop it.

Julian   You want to be liked.

Bea   He needs to get laid.

Stew (*sobs*)   Ohhhhhh! A girl. A woman. Someone to like me.

Bea   Fuck you, you mean.

Mrs Snowball   Swearing, again!

Linda   Excuse me, this is a vicarage!

Bea   Yeah, and this is a fish paste sandwich.

Julian   India, it's alright. This is a free space.

Stew   I need help.

Julian   You are loved.

Bea   He doesn't love him. He wants his soul.

Linda   Why have you come here? To attack Alex? He's a good man, a loving man.

Bea   They took my baby off me. The church stole my child.

Mrs Snowball   I'll go t'foot of our stairs! They took her bain off of her.

Linda   You were an unmarried mother?

Julian   Where was this, Moss?

Bea   England. I was scum to you. A sinner. A slag. Unfit to be a mother.

Julian   Is that why you steal?

Bea   I don't steal.

Julian   There were two silver candlesticks on the mantelpiece earlier. They've gone. You've not taken your big jacket off.

Bea   All property is theft.

Moss grabs Italian Dave, who is still kneeling, by the collar and hauls him upright.

Bea   You! Dave! Come on. You're coming home with me. These two need to be alone. Get that jar.

Stew   This?

Linda   That's the fund for the bells.

Bea   The vodka fund.

Julian   Moss, please –

Bea   – you stole my baby!

Italian Dave pockets a sandwich and some biscuits.

Stew   Thanks for the sarnies.

Moss and Italian Dave leave.

Linda   Who is your house open to?

Enter a **Taxi Driver** *into the house using a vom.*

Taxi Driver   Taxi for Mrs Snowball! Hermioni Snowball. (*Pronounced 'hermeowni'.*)

Mrs Snowball   Hermioni! We're coming. Hermeeoni? Didn't you ever go to school.

Taxi Driver   I did yeah. Twice.

Mrs Snowball *runs down to the stage with Our* **Seth** *and goes to exit using the stage door.*

Mrs Snowball   Come on, our Seth! I asked for a lady driver.

Taxi Driver   I have a licence.

Mrs Snowball   To be a woman?

Taxi Driver   You can trust me.

Mrs Snowball   It's not you I'm worried about, love.

Linda (*as* **Seth** *passes her*)   Hello, our Seth.

Seth   Hello, Linda. Have you gorra boyfriend?

Mrs Snowball   C'mon, our Seth. (*She heads for the onstage exit.*)

Julian   That doesn't go anywhere.

Mrs Snowball   They went out that way!

Taxi Driver   I'm over here.

Seth   This way, Mam!

Mrs Snowball   What a load of filthy tripe!

They're gone.

Linda   You're a good man. A beautiful man.

Julian   Just us then, now. Shall I put the kettle on?

Seth (*off*)   If you think it'll go with your outfit.

She puts a hand out to him, stroking his hair. They kiss passionately.

Linda   Shall we go upstairs?

Julian   Yes. But one thing.

Linda   What's that?

Julian   I'd better lock the door.

Bea *and* **Stew** *enter in cassocks with instruments.*

Julian's Song

(*Singing*)
   The power of the lord is truly awesome
   Truly awesome, truly awesome
   The power of the lord is truly awesome
   And he sent his son to save our souls

The bread we love is the body of christ
The body of christ, the body of christ
The bread we love is the body of christ
Fresh from skeltons on Bev Road

The wine we drink is the blood of the lord
The blood of the lord, the blood of the lord
The wine we drink is the blood of the lord
Valpolicella from the spa

All that he asks is that we learn to love him
Learn to love him, learn to love him
All that he asks is that we learn to love him
And he'll wangle you eternal life

Our love making is a gift to the lord
A gift to the lord, a gift to the lord
Our love making is a gift to the lord
And the giving goes on all day

Our souls, our souls, our souls, our souls.

The Critics

The set of the play in full lights. They're taking it down, doing the get out, so in and out, all carrying props or bits of flats, furniture.

Julian (*reading*) 'The revolutionary theatre troupe, Hull Truck' –

Linda – Mike won't like that.

Bea Are we revolutionary?

Stew Our aims are different from most theatre companies. We want to piss people off and empty the theatre by the interval.

Enter **Bradwell**.

Bradwell What's this? A review?

Bea Man or woman, reviewing?

Julian Theodore Basset.

Stew Reviewed by a dog!

Julian Bassets are hounds.

Bradwell It's endless, innit.

Julian It's not correct to describe a basset hound as a dog. They're bred to hunt, so bassets are hounds.

Stew Read the bloody review!

Bradwell No. Wait until I'm out the room. We did what I wanted to do. For me it was brilliant. The critics can go to hell. What paper is it?

Julian *East Hull Advertiser*.

Bradwell I'm not interested. *West Hull Advertiser*, possibly. I want you to learn to rise above the approval of others.

Stew Oooh.

Bradwell   To avoid criticism, do nothing, say nothing, be nothing.

Bea   My agent says a critic is someone who knows the way, but can't drive.

Stew   Come on, read it!

Bradwell *puts his fingers in his ears and hums a low hum.*

Julian (*reading*)   – 'Hull Truck brought the language of the factory to the stage in this plotless drama which was little more than an excuse for a lot of bad behaviour. I lost count of the number of times the F word was used as a lazy intensifier.'

Stew   They sent a hound that can't count?!

Bradwell *grabs one end of the sofa.*

Bradwell   Stew, get on the end of this.

They lift the sofa and head off out.

Julian   Mrs Snowball and Seth enjoyed it.

Bea   'There's no need to swear!'

Julian   But that's fantastic. Isn't it?

Linda   Engaging an audience with matters that are important to them.

Bea (*surreptitiously*)   I might have to talk to my agent.

Julian   No! The play we made together is unique.

Bea   Thank God. No one wants two plays like that.

Julian (*to* **Linda**)   Did I see Gillian Diamond talking to you last night?

Linda   Yes.

Julian   Thanks for introducing me.

Linda   She couldn't hang around, someone had offered her a lift.

Bea   Gillian Diamond?

Julian   Casting director of the Royal Court. She touched your arm, I saw her.

Bea   Bit intimate. That's gotta be good.

Julian   I've seen some terrible shit at the Royal Court.

Linda   Yes!

Enter **Bradwell** *and* **Stew**.

Bradwell   Radical suggestion. How to do a get out. Get three actors to stand around gassing about their careers and let the director do it all on his tod.

This fires the others into action. All three pick up something and head off to the van.

Stew   Mike?

Bradwell   What?

Stew   I've got an audition, a telly.

Bradwell   Telly? Telly? What television?

Stew   A crime thing.

Bradwell   Soap or one off?

Stew   Police 5.

Bradwell   Police 5? The crime reconstruction show.

Stew   I'm the spitting image of a some Welsh bank robber.

Bradwell   Good money?

Stew   Robbing banks? Gotta be.

Bradwell   If you look like the guy, why do they need to audition you?

Stew   They don't.

Bradwell   They've given you the job and you don't have the balls to fess up.

Stew   That's it! Exactly.

Bradwell   Congratulations.

Stew   Thanks.

Bradwell   Go on then. Fuck off.

Stew   Now?

Bradwell   Yeah.

Stew   Ta. See you. I've learned a lot. From you. About er –

Bradwell   – fuck off.

Stew   Acting. Truthful acting.

Stew *is gone.* **Bradwell** *pauses for a beat,* **Julian** *comes back in.*

Julian   Do you have a moment?

Bradwell   'I want to be a writer'.

Julian   Yes. The sermon I wrote . . . I loved the process, sitting in a room, on my own, it is the quintessence of me. I've found myself. I'm not letting you down, Mike. They've cancelled the run and we don't have another booking.

Bradwell   You're an annoying, clever, fucking knowitall. Writing might suit you. Go on, fuck off.

Julian *picks up a chair and looks at* **Bradwell**.

Julian   We're going to the Polar Bear.

Bradwell   See you in there.

Julian   Pint of cheap lager.

Bradwell   Not necessarily cheap.

Julian I'm buying. I shall miss Hull. Coltman Street. Buying one egg. The Polar Bear. Gwenap.

Julian *picks up one of two remaining chairs.*

Just these?

Bradwell I've got 'em.

Julian *puts the chair down, and leaves.* **Bradwell** *sits on the chair. He wraps his arm around his head as his wont. Enter* **Linda**.

Linda The Royal Court were in last night. They want me to audition. Meet some directors.

Bradwell Of course they do.

Linda I feel as if I'm betraying something. This, us, you, I dunno.

Bradwell The Royal Court is your favourite theatre. You must go.

Linda I –

Bradwell – go! It's all a caper.

Linda *kisses his forehead and leaves. Enter* **Howard Gibbins**, *carrying a* Guardian.

Bradwell We're out of here. No need to give me a bollocking.

Gibbins I don't work for the theatre. Not this one. Howard Gibbins. I run the Bush in London.

Bradwell The Bush Theatre?

Gibbins You know it?

Bradwell Shepherd's Bush. Irish pub. Fight every night. Broken toilets.

Gibbins I always go before I leave the house. I was in last night.

They shake hands.

Bradwell   You hated it?

Gibbins   I adored it.

Bradwell   What's wrong with you, then?

Gibbins   I'm not the only one. Robin Thornber?

Bradwell   The twat who writes for the *Guardian*.

Gibbins   You don't read the *Guardian*?

Bradwell   Do I look like a *Guardian* reader? They won't be happy until we're all as miserable as they are.

Gibbins   I'll read it to you. Do you mind?

Gibbins *sits*.

Bradwell   When was Thornber in?

Gibbins   Tuesday.

Bradwell   Did he leave at the interval?

Gibbins (*reading*)   'There were less than fifty people dotted about the Gulbenkian theatre last night for the opening of Hull Truck's show *Naked*. At the end only twenty-two remained. One brave lady stormed out shouting 'filthy tripe!' This was presumably because the script was liberally sprinkled with a word that rhymes with Truck that you never hear on the telly but you do hear in most situations where passionate people are being honest with each other. Tripe is dull, flabby, and lifeless. *Naked* is lively, tough, full of surprises, truth and comedy. It offers no pat answers, it doesn't assault us with liberal values, but it does ask all the right questions about what it is to be human. A huge achievement. Keep on trucking.'

Bradwell   I might start reading the *Guardian*.

Gibbins   It's only a newspaper.

Bradwell   And tonight's fish wrapper.

Gibbins   I have a slot in March –

Bradwell   – you mean, for us to bring this show to you. To the Bush? In London?

Gibbins   You're a touring theatre aren't you?

Bradwell   Yes, we make the work here in Hull, and then we tour it. We're staying in Hull.

Gibbins   Why Hull?

Bradwell   Because it's a bit shit and completely fucking brilliant at the same time and –

Gibbins   – and?

Bradwell   It keeps you real.

Gibbins   As an artist? How does it do that?

Bradwell   If you think you're being clever and weird, you take a look out the window. Hull is one great big outdoor asylum.

Gibbins   What's your philosophy? Of theatre?

Bradwell   Hull Fair with tits.

Gibbins   Who do I negotiate contracts with? Do you have a business exec?

Bradwell   Yes. No. It's all me.

Gibbins   My card.

He stands.

Gotta go. I'm chasing a train back to London. What's your number?

Bradwell   What's my phone number?

Gibbins   You don't have a telephone?

Bradwell   There is a telephone. I'll write the number down for you.

He writes it down on a torn in half beer mat. **Gibbins** *gives him a pen.*

Bradwell   When you ring, let it ring. Just . . . you know, just let it ring and ring.

Gibbins   Keep it ringing?

Bradwell   Kind of, yeah. Eventually someone, someone in Hull will answer it.

They shake hands. **Gibbins** *turns to leave, stops.*

Gibbins   It's not a theatre town, is it?

Bradwell   City.

Gibbins   City, is it? Sorry. Do you think Hull Truck will be here in fifty years' time?

Bradwell   I fucking hope not.

Gibbins *leaves.* **Bradwell** *sits on the chair. He looks at the card, puts it in his pocket. He stands, picks up the two remaining chairs and leaves closing the bay doors after him.*

Lights fade.

The End.

Curtain.

Reprise 'Que Sera, Sera'.

9 781350 342125